D1498116

GREAT LAKES
FOR SALE

GREAT LAKES
FOR SALE

FROM WHITECAPS TO BOTTLECAPS

Dave Dempsey

With a Foreword by
Congressman Bart Stupak

THE UNIVERSITY OF MICHIGAN PRESS / ANN ARBOR *and*
THE PETOSKEY PUBLISHING COMPANY / TRAVERSE CITY

Published in the United States of America by
The University of Michigan Press
and
The Petoskey Publishing Company
Manufactured in the United States of America
⊛ Printed on acid-free paper

2011   2010   2009   2008   4 3 2 1

A CIP catalog record for this book is available from the British Library.

Library of Congress Cataloging-in-Publication Data

Dempsey, Dave, 1957–
    Great Lakes for sale : from whitecaps to bottlecaps / Dave Dempsey.
        p.   cm.
    Includes index.
    ISBN-13: 978-0-472-11649-2 (cloth : alk. paper)
    ISBN-10: 0-472-11649-5 (cloth : alk. paper)
        1. Water resources development—Great Lakes Region (North
America)   2. Water-supply—Great Lakes (North America)—Management.
I. Title.

    HD1694.A2D46   2008
    333.91'630977—dc22   2007052491

A Caravan book. For more information,
visit www.caravanbooks.org.

To the courageous members of

Michigan Citizens for Water Conservation,

Especially Terry and Gary Swier,

And attorney Jim Olson.

Future generations will thank you.

The Great Lakes already do.

Foreword

AS THE ONLY MEMBER of the U.S. House of Representatives with a district touching three of the five Great Lakes, I have a special interest in what happens to these precious waters. The people of my district in northern Michigan care deeply about the Great Lakes. The Great Lakes support our spectacular sport fishery, provide a route for commercial and recreational navigation, and supply many communities with drinking water. Water means jobs and life in my district.

In the Congress, I have fought federal proposals to allow the dumping of sewage into our lakes, have supported reaffirmation of our successful Clean Water Act, and have formed a Congressional Water Caucus.

I am deeply concerned about the future of freshwater itself. As sources of freshwater become more limited in the twenty-first century, concerns have been raised that the Great Lakes will be the solution to other areas' water problems. Back in 1998, the Nova Group of Sault Sainte Marie, Ontario, proposed to sell water in bulk from the Great Lakes for export to Asia. I was able to lead the fight to stop the proposed shipments, but this scheme made it very clear that stronger water guidelines need to be put in place.

The intent of the proposed Great Lakes Basin compact that is now before the Great Lakes states for ratification is to prevent diversion of this precious resource. This means that we must follow through with wise use and conservation measures and not just articulate a plan. We must have accurate and up-to-date data gathered by all participating users of Great Lakes water.

The goal, in my judgment, is not just to limit water diversions to other states in the United States but also to develop a basinwide standard that will be strong enough to stand up to international trade laws.

Recent marketing of Great Lakes water for sale, like the Nestlé operations in Michigan, points out the urgency of the need for a basinwide standard for withdrawals. Commoditization of Great Lakes water for sale will continue to be an enormous issue. Because commoditization can create enormous problems with international trade agreements and North American Free Trade Agreement (NAFTA) policies, there must be a comprehensive, basinwide policy to prevent the creation of precedents and vested rights.

The last thing I want to see is international or foreign companies in control of our Great Lakes water under trade laws and treaties. I spoke about this in the congressional debates on NAFTA in 1993, but few people were listening.

Dave Dempsey's book is an important part of the effort to remind people why commercialization of Great Lakes water is a dangerous threat. It's not simply a matter of how much water in the short term is bottled and shipped away; the long-term threat is control of water and the possibility that private interests will assert ownership of the very substance of the Great Lakes. This is an issue that could determine the fate of the Great Lakes. I encourage the millions who care about the Great Lakes to read and act on this valuable book.

Our Great Lakes water must always remain a public resource in public hands. It's a matter of prosperity, fairness, and survival.

Congressman Bart Stupak
First District, Michigan

Acknowledgments

ONE OF THE MOST important lessons of a career spent working (not always successfully) on government policy is that the vast majority of Americans speak a different language from the policy population in Washington, D.C., and state capitals. Their parlance is generally clear, punchy, and linked to daily stresses, needs and joys. Meanwhile, we policy people not only use a five-syllable vocabulary when one-syllable words will do just fine, but we can't even explain what should be simple ideas—for example, why it is not a good thing to let corporations make increasingly bold ownership claims on the public's waters, including the Great Lakes.

To the extent that this book makes that idea more clear and persuasive, the credit goes to my good friend Jennifer Morris, who kindly but clearly let me know that my early attempts to explain the concept were not meeting the standard of effective communication. So as I wrote this, I kept in mind the words "short and sweet" and "to the point."

The same public policy career has brought me in touch with many remarkable people whose commitment to a sustainable society and a healthy planet helps many of us keep going. To name just a few, these include Tom Bailey of Petoskey, Michigan, a genuine Teddy Roosevelt Republican; Sandy Bihn of Oregon, Ohio, who is also the western Lake Erie waterkeeper; Michelle Hurd Riddick and David Riddick of Saginaw, Michigan, who won't settle for anything but clean Great Lakes, and a clean Saginaw Bay watershed; Mark Van Putten of Virginia, the former executive director of the National Wildlife Federation and a Michigan conservation legend; and Joan and Willard Wolfe of Frankfort, Michigan, who have done so much to protect the Great Lakes and to keep alive the dream of an enduring Michigan.

I want to give thanks to several people who assisted in the development of this book, patiently answering questions and offering insights when requested—or simply holding the line on principle when the commercialization of water became a looming legal possibility. A few of these people include Wisconsin water guru Peter McAvoy, environmental attorney Jim Olson, and Cooley Law School professor Chris Shafer. In tough times, David Holtz and Cyndi Roper of Clean Water Action in Michigan kept the faith on the policy goal of keeping water a public and not a private resource, and helped me to believe that our Great Lakes might not be put up for sale. Brian McKenna offered an example of Irish steadfastness and scholarship over the months this book came together. My apologies to the many others that I've overlooked.

The Michigan Environmental Council, long my professional home, and its many outstanding staff members will always have my respect.

My gratitude also goes to Mary Erwin, the Associate Director of the University of Michigan Press, who has patiently awaited this manuscript, critiqued it constructively, and helped bring it to publication.

Thanks also to friends and heroes Kathleen Aterno, Tom Baldini, Leslie Brogan, Lois Debacker, Patrick Diehl, Tracy Dobson, Marty Fluharty, Elizabeth Harris, Carol Misseldine, Lana Pollack, Skip Pruss, Darlene Durrwachter Rushing and Derwin Rushing, Margaret Schulte, Tom Vance, Bronwyn Jones and Joe VanderMeulen, and Lisa Wyatt Knowlton.

Finally, I'm grateful to some Minnesota friends who have helped introduce me to the wonders of the land of 10,000 (actually 11,842) Lakes: Paul Austin, Scott Banas, Whitney Clark, Lani Jordan, Gayle Peterson, and Ron Kroese.

None of these people shoulder any responsibility for errors or imprecision in what follows. But all of them, in some way, helped give me the strength to write it in the first place.

Contents

"I am afraid that I don't see much hope for a civilization so stupid that it demands a quantitative estimate of the value of its own umbilical cord."

—Dr. David Ehrenfeld, Rutgers University

Prologue

IN THE GRAINY black-and-white snapshots, whose ends are now curled with age, three young brothers under the age of seven with crew cuts stand squinting and smiling in the shallow water off a Lake Michigan beach. One of the boys—me—has what would be termed a beer belly in an adult and is gleefully unconscious of the fact. Wearing shoulder-strap undershirts and swim trunks, the boys are facing landward for the photographer, their father or mother. Behind them is a tinted gray horizon unbroken by waves or the sight of land. In the snapshots, time has stopped in 1962; like summer, the Great Lakes are eternal.

So we all thought, those of us who grew up among the Great Lakes or visited them as children. *They've always been here, and they always will be.*

Only as adults did we acquire the statistics that struggled to express that childhood wonder at Great Lakes water.

- 18 percent of the world's available surface freshwater
- Enough water, if the lakes were spilled out like a pitcher, to cover the 48 contiguous states to a depth of 9.5 feet
- Six quadrillion gallons of water
- 95 percent of the available surface freshwater of the United States
- 10 percent of the world's available surface freshwater in one lake (Superior)
- 10,900 miles of U.S. and Canadian Great Lakes shoreline

It is the curse of adulthood—and politics—to need numbers to justify what the heart knows: that there are no lakes like the Great Lakes, no place like the Great Lakes, and no freshwater more worth defending than the Great Lakes.

Numbers are also the province of politics and economics. Wonder has no dollar value. Eternity cannot be quantified. So it happens that in the equations of public policy—including environmental statutes and cost-benefit analyses—the majesty, lineage, and future of the Great Lakes carry no weight.

I've seen how this plays out.

For a quarter century, as a professional environmental advocate in and out of government, I've been inspired to tears, laughter, rage, and hope by the powerful and often unscripted oratory of citizens fighting a toxic dump, warring on behalf of an ancient sand dune, pleading for the protection of their child's health from a proposed smokestack, or begging for the protection of a last stand of Pitcher's thistle on a threatened Great Lakes beach. But I've also anticipated, after the first few such speeches, the response of the government officials sitting at the front of the auditorium or meeting room and recording public comment: *We understand your concern, but you need to understand the law and deal with the facts, not emotions.*

And after 25 years I've seen where that leads us: not to a recovering, healthful, natural world and habitat for human beings but to its lingering death by a hundred million cuts.

Not even the Great Lakes can take a hundred million cuts and survive. But that's what they're being asked to do. That's what many of my professional, principled colleagues in the environmental movement are asking them to do. That's what government regulators are asking them to do. Most of all, that's what the "rational actors" of business and industry are asking them do—in the face of hard-won education about the vulnerability of the Great Lakes.

We have to deal with the facts, not the emotions, when it comes to the Great Lakes, they say.

All right, then, I'll give you the facts. But I won't deny the emotions. If those of us who grew up with potbellies—standing in sweet waters on hot summer days wondering at the seeming infinity of the Lakes—start relying solely on facts, that's the end of the Great Lakes and so much else.

The game of environmental protection, and Great Lakes protection, is rigged by those who would profit and not well defended by those in government who would act as referees over the plunder of our own home.

One fact is that the Great Lakes are in grave danger in an era of globalization and commercialization. That's what this book is about. That—and all the priceless memories of a hundred million childhoods past and future.

Among the world's available surface freshwater, 18 percent is harbored by the Great Lakes. Is 18 percent of humankind's responsibility for freshwater harbored by the people of the Great Lakes? These people of the basin amount to about *one-half of one percent* of the world's human population after all.[1] So they face a burden 36 times larger than they should be asked to bear. Isn't that a tall order to demand from them?

I don't think so—but we'll all find out soon.

T. Boone Pickens, the Dallas hedge fund manager and oil billionaire, spent more than $50 million for water rights around his 24,000-acre ranch in North Texas. He says he has enough water to serve 20 percent of the Dallas–Fort Worth area. So far, Pickens, 78, has failed to convince any Texas cities to buy his water, and he needs a commitment before he can build a $2 billion pipeline system.

Water is a finite resource that will only become more expensive, Pickens said in a June 16 interview in New York. He compared the demand for water to China's purchases of oil fields from Canada to Kazakhstan, saying, "I'd be the same way about water."

—Bloomberg News, July 3, 2006

CHAPTER 1

Stumbling Toward a Charter

IT WAS NOVEMBER of 1983, and most of the Great Lakes region was struggling to recover from the near depression of the previous years. In Michigan, unemployment had climbed to 17 percent only 12 months earlier. So when a batch of newly elected Great Lakes governors met in Indianapolis, regional economic competition and growth were high on the agenda. As an aide to the governor of Michigan, I had one aim: to cinch agreement among the chief executives on the request from my boss to deal with one of the most critical long-term economic issues facing the region.

The chief result: Democratic Michigan governor James J. Blanchard got what he wanted. The eight governors or their representatives agreed to set up a task force on how to prevent the draining of the Great Lakes.

Looking back on two and a half decades of talk about the issue of Great Lakes water exports, it's critical to observe that in the compartmentalized world of public policy it was the further loss of jobs, not the risk of environmental catastrophe, that characterized the issue. Environmental policy aides and water law experts were nominally in charge of developing the governors' plan to protect the Great Lakes, but the saliency of the issue to the public, and hence the politicians, derived chiefly from the nightmare of additional economic erosion to the oil-producing, temperate Sunbelt states.

What worried the Great Lakes public in 1983 was the mental image of a giant pipeline, reaching from, say, the south end of Lake Michigan to

Texas, fueling the rapid economic expansion of the Southwest. Prohibitively expensive, an engineering feat of monumental proportions, and decades away from reality at best, the image was nonetheless compelling. It played to our region's sense of abandonment by the nation after putting America on wheels and serving as the central arsenal of democracy in World War II. The Sunbelt would drain not just our population but also our distinguishing natural resource—water. We were not about to let that happen.

Some would call that economic protectionism, and it's true that the Great Lakes then and now have a great deal to do with the economy of their surrounding states and Canadian provinces. In the 1980s, the rule was that each inch by which one of the Great Lakes fell cost commercial shippers $50 million in lost cargo capacity. Availability of water as a transport route, a raw material, and the heart of the ecosystem had contributed to the emergence of the steel, auto, and chemical industries in the early 1900s, the prosperity of agriculture, the sportfishing boom begun in the 1960s, and the expansion of tourism. Restaurants, hotels, cottages, resorts, marinas, and more depended on the lakes. Sucking them up, even in part, would undermine that residue of the region's economic base.

At least two paper plans to begin the draining of the lakes had set off an alarm. A $2.1 billion scheme to construct a coal slurry pipeline from the Powder River Basin in Wyoming and Montana to Duluth, using Lake Superior water to suspend the coal, excited concerns in the late 1970s and early 1980s. The International Joint Commission, a treaty organization created by Canada and the United States, concluded that the impact would be minimal—less than 1 percent of the Chicago diversion—if any Lake Superior water would be needed at all.[1] Ultimately the project failed on economic grounds.

The bigger insult to the pride of the Great Lakes states was delivered in 1982 when, under a mandate from the U.S. Congress, the Army Corps of Engineers studied the feasibility of diverting the Great Lakes to replenish water supplies in the agricultural region served by the once-vast Ogallala Aquifer, which underlies some of the nation's most productive farmland. Although the study did not support the economics of the proposal and the corps didn't recommend moving forward, the review spooked Great Lakes citizens and the politicians who represented them.[2] That's where Michigan governor Blanchard stepped in to call for the regional task force.

There was another, less dramatic but also national impulse behind the concern about Great Lakes water exports. In 1982, in a case involving ranchers who owned contiguous land in both Colorado and Nebraska and wanted to overturn Nebraska's ban on the export of groundwater to another state, the U.S. Supreme Court ruled that water was not just the source of life but also an article of interstate commerce "similar to wheat or steel," as one analyst put it. (Ten years later, the court would confirm in a Michigan case that household garbage belongs on the list of articles of interstate commerce along with water.) Unless Congress explicitly delegated the power to regulate commerce in water to the states, the court held, state export bans not related expressly to the legitimate policing-power purposes of water conservation or water resource preservation would not stand.

And so, as the task force advising the Council of Great Lakes Governors began its work in late 1983, two forces were about to collide. The region's citizens and politicians wanted a way to just say no to water exports. But the task force, peering at the Supreme Court decision, decided it needed to tailor restrictions to meet a much more complicated design—water conservation. Otherwise, the Supreme Court would ultimately strike down the enactment of its recommendations. The task force would have to come up with rules that would, instead of banning water exports, *authorize* them under certain select, though infrequent, circumstances. Those circumstances couldn't be too far-fetched or speculative lest the Supreme Court call the rules a ban in disguise.

To make matters even more complicated, the task force had the job of coming up with an ecological rationale for limiting exports of the world's most abundant freshwater resource. It would literally have to show how and why resource conservation, not protectionism, was the basis for action by the Great Lakes states—even though enough water filled the lakes to make the continental United States into a swimming pool. Difficult enough in any case, the job was made tougher by the fact that most of the Great Lakes states had no statutory restrictions on the in-state use of water. They would have to persuade the Supreme Court someday that they simply wanted to use water wisely while they exercised no control over water use within their boundaries.

And nowhere was this contradiction more clear than in Michigan, whose license plates boldly proclaimed it to be the Great Lakes state.

Michigan, 99.9 percent of which benefits from and drains into the Great Lakes, had no meaningful statutory law promoting water conservation. Why should it? Generations of lawmakers and citizens had asked that question. *We're surrounded by so much water we don't know what to do with all of it.*

Enter Thomas L. Washington, the executive director of an organization that terrified politicians, the Michigan United Conservation Clubs (MUCC). Born from the anger of sportsmen in the late 1930s about the threat of a return to the political spoils system that had permitted the ravaging of Michigan's forests, fish, and game, MUCC had fought ever since—at least in theory—to make sure Michigan's conservation agencies thought about long-term values, not immediate electoral rewards for governors and legislators. In 1976, just six years before the election of my boss, Blanchard, MUCC had claimed the lion's share of the credit for defying the legislature and collecting more than 300,000 petition signatures to place on the November ballot a law requiring deposits on beer and soda containers—an antilitter, prorecycling initiative opposed by beer and wine wholesalers and store operators. Voters had approved the MUCC law by a whopping margin. And that scared the politicians.

In July 1983, after joining the governor's staff, I began regular visits to Mr. Washington's office. I'll never forget them. The first time, after waiting an appropriate length of time in his receptionist's office, I was ushered into his sanctum. I moved briskly to a chair in front of his massive desk as he greeted me and tapped a cigarette out of its pack. He lit it and puffed. I waited for him, sensing but not yet really grasping the furnishings around me. After repeated visits I'd develop an inventory: the bearskin rug, the stuffed African primate holding a roll of toilet paper between its stilled hands, the deer hoof ashtray. During our talks Washington would remain seated, sometimes sipping coffee from an incongruous fine cup and saucer, sniffing at me when I said something naive but generally remaining congenial.

Not long after the Council of Great Lakes Governors announced the creation of its task force to come up with a legally defensible strategy to save the waters of the lakes, and even closer to the day when Governor Blanchard (on my recommendation) named a University of Michigan environmental law expert, Joseph L. Sax, to represent the state on the task force, Washington brought up the subject. I don't read people well now, and was even worse at it in 1983. When he said he had problems with the governor's initiative, I wasn't sure what he meant. Obviously Tom Washington and MUCC wanted to stop the draining of the Great Lakes. Then what did they object to?

A polite phone call from a typically very outspoken staff ecologist for MUCC, Wayne Schmidt, educated me a bit. It turned out that Joe Sax and Tom Washington had collided over a major 1970s environmental issue of which I knew little. Sax had argued with eloquence and passion for the protection from oil and gas drilling of the Pigeon River Country State Forest, a stunning wild area cultivated by thoughtful foresters and administrators after the timber ravaging of the late 1800s. Washington had cut a deal with the oil and gas industry permitting limited drilling in exchange for the dedication of oil and gas revenues from drilling on state lands to a special fund used to purchase public recreational land. The two men had sparred angrily in public over the deal. Wayne politely suggested that I might have done a little research on this before recommending Joe Sax even though Wayne respected Sax's intelligence and legal scholarship.

That was blunder number one. It wouldn't be the last.

Well into 1984, Professor Sax, who quickly commanded the respect of the others on the task force with his understanding of constitutional law and his commitment to the public trust doctrine (more on that later), kept me informed of his work on behalf of the state. He was careful to let me know that he was determined to craft a strategy that would stand up in the U.S. Supreme Court and would protect the Great Lakes for all time. That wouldn't mean an embargo on water exports, he reminded me. It would set rules, based on defensible science and law, for any withdrawals or exports that might someday occur. In doing so it would meet the test of evenhandedness sought by the Supreme Court. The Founders, clearly, had not intended that regions of the United States would put up economic walls; this was one nation, and its prosperity could best be assured through national, not multiple regional, superintendents.

I recognized what he was saying but had to reflect on how differently Tom Washington thought and felt. In one of our conversations he had said words to the effect, "The Great Lakes can't be protected by half measures. We either stand up and say 'not a drop leaves the basin' or we lose control for good." Implicit in his words was not just a hard-knuckled political sensibility but also a native's sense of attachment to the holy waters. Washington and Sax had essentially traded places from the Pigeon River debate: the MUCC head opposed any compromise while the environmental law expert saw it as the only way to protect the lakes from being drained.

It was fortunate, for me at least, that a governor of a state like Michigan has more important things to do than accept daily, weekly, or even monthly briefings from a staff aide on such matters as a Great Lakes task force. I could ponder the temperamental and rational differences between Sax and Washington at my leisure without having to disturb the chief executive of the state with them. I could also defer the day of reckoning for me. In the spirit of all long-serving political aides over the eons, I hoped to find a way to bridge the gap. My vision, though never so explicit, was a news conference where Governor Blanchard, Joe Sax, and Tom Washington would declare with pride that Michigan had stood up for the Great Lakes, which would be defended in perpetuity by a strategy on which the three men agreed.

That day never arrived. As 1984 wore on and the interstate task force began to develop its recommendations to the governors, I wondered how I could get the governor and myself out of the mess I had created. I hadn't thought through the legal and political issues. As Professor Sax continued to brief me, I realized he was captaining a report that Tom Washington would condemn to any reporter that would listen. The governor was about to take a political beating from the most important conservation group in the state less than two years before his reelection campaign. And most of Michigan's electorate would agree with Washington: why would their governor tolerate a proposal that would allow some water to be taken from the lakes for other regions, including, perhaps, the Sunbelt?

Although I sweated over it, I ultimately decided there was only one proper course for the interests of the governor: he would have to reject the idea of setting rules on when Great Lakes water could be exported. This is where memory blurs. I'm not sure—and am doubtful—that I directly said this to Professor Sax. My recollection is that I hinted at it and when presented with his draft recommendations edited them to reflect a "no exports" position.

I must have sent the paper back to him because somewhere around Christmas 1984 I received a phone call from a reporter for the *Detroit News*. "Dave," the reporter said incredulously, "Joe Sax has resigned." My heart nearly seized. There was nothing I could do but mumble the trite generalities that all politicos rely on: the governor was grateful for the professor's service, but on the governor's behalf I wasn't sure he could support the recommendations of the interstate task force. Professor Sax was in the right, I knew: I'd put him, as well as the governor, in an impossible position.

The other Great Lakes states and Ontario weren't happy, either. After spending a year on a report commissioned by Michigan, they were now being asked to embrace a revised version that would not commit the Great Lakes state to the enactment of a statute permitting water use. I accepted a series of phone calls from members of the task force who wondered whether they were being sandbagged.

I told them there was still great value in moving ahead with the report. At least it bound all eight Great Lakes states and the provinces of Ontario and Quebec in a common accord on management of major new water withdrawals and diversions. The revised proposal would oblige each signatory to give notice to all the others whenever such withdrawals or diversions were proposed and to consider (though not necessarily heed) comments or objections from the others. This "good neighbor" rule would put into action a concept at the center of Great Lakes management since the previous decade—ecosystem management. It would also expressly state that the chief executives of all 10 jurisdictions held the lakes to be "precious public natural resources, shared and held in trust by the Great Lakes States and Provinces." And, although it wouldn't commit anyone to the enactment of new laws, it would strongly hint at the necessity of doing so: "In recognition of their shared responsibility to conserve and protect the water resources of the Great Lakes Basin for the use, benefit, and enjoyment of all their citizens, the States and Provinces agree to seek (where necessary) and to implement legislation establishing programs to manage and regulate the diversion and consumptive use of Basin water resources."

It was a step forward in other words. And the other jurisdictions reluctantly agreed.

If I thought all of this would be enough to calm down Tom Washington, I was wrong. (For one thing, you never "calmed down" Washington any more than you calmed down a hurricane. Both forces have to spend themselves.) The revised agreement, now called the Great Lakes Charter, certainly suggested that Michigan needed to produce a law that would allow the issuance of permits for some water diversions. In the fine print, which Washington and his adviser Schmidt read, the charter said that states or provinces that didn't have laws giving them the authority to "manage and regulate" diversions and withdrawals averaging 2 million gallons or more per day were not entitled to prior notice and consultation by the others. This meant that unless Michigan passed such a law it might be ignored in regional conferences on major new water uses.

Subsequently MUCC launched an all-out offensive against Michigan's participation in the charter. Washington personally appeared before the chief governing body of the Michigan Department of Natural Resources (DNR), the Natural Resources Commission, to urge the seven members to advise against the charter, calling it a betrayal of the Great Lakes. On behalf of Governor Blanchard, I appeared before the commission to urge just the opposite, and I was able to tell the members that former governor William G. Milliken, a much-loved Republican who had retired at the end of 1982, also supported the charter. In a phone call placed not long before the commission met, the former governor had graciously expressed his view that regional unity of purpose on the water export issue was worth any minor compromise in the charter. The commission agreed—perhaps influenced in part by the fact that its members are appointed by the governor of Michigan.

And so, in the teeth of opposition from the state's largest conservation group, Governor Blanchard prepared to join his executive colleagues in Milwaukee in mid-February 1985 to sign the charter to national fanfare. Flying over a frozen Lake Michigan with a pleased Governor Blanchard that morning, I felt relief and a faint exaltation. But I also wondered whether Tom Washington and MUCC's gut instinct might have had more legal support than I supposed. At any rate, the decision on whether Michigan could take a tougher line on water diversions could be studied, and handled, another day. For now, preserving a still-fragile Great Lakes regional unity was more important. The road to the charter had been rocky, full of potholes resulting from my naïveté and inexperience, but the journey had been worth it. Not waiting for Washington and Ottawa to work their inscrutable—and perhaps hostile—will on the lakes, the states and provinces were beginning to undertake stewardship of the great waters.

As the photographers snapped pictures and reporters jotted down the scripted quotes of the governors and premiers that morning, it felt like history had been made.

Unfortunately, it would be the first of several Great Lakes agreements and laws that would prove less sturdy in practice than they seemed on paper.

On the first camping trip of my life in the summer of 1981, at the age of 24, half a dozen environmental advocates from the Sierra Club persuaded me to strap on a backpack and walk eastward with them into the backcountry of the Pictured Rocks National Lakeshore in Michigan. As we neared our campsite on the overnight excursion, the sky over Lake Superior, to our left, grew troubled, and thunder rolled far out over the waters. The storm bypassed our resting place, and soon the clouds yielded to brilliant evening sun.

That night I slept for the first time in a tent. After adjusting to the feeling of a thin air mattress below and thin roof above, I fell asleep. I awoke at sunrise to hear a rhythmic pounding, like the slap of a giant hand on a drum.

Boom . . . boom . . . boom.

Pulling on my sweatshirt and jeans, I struggled out of the tent and wandered, slack jawed, to the edge of the great bluff overlooking Superior. No one else in our party was yet awake, leaving me alone to stare at the frigid blue waters, which reached to the north like a yearning for eternity. The early morning sunlight broke into little shards of white glass on the tops of the waves that slammed against the base of the bluff.

I thought: I want people 100 years from now, 500 years from now, to be able to behold and admire this same scene.

After considering journalism and teaching, I now knew what my life's work would be. I knew also I would never forget this moment.

CHAPTER 2

Public Trust, but Verify

ONE DAY DURING THE beastly hot, drought-plagued early summer of 1988, Governor Blanchard exclaimed in a meeting with several staff that at Fourth of July parades and other public events he was hearing more spontaneous remarks from citizens than ever before about the need to protect the Great Lakes from being drained. In 1985, near record high lake levels had washed coastal homes into surging waters and prompted Michigan to spend tens of millions of dollars on shoreline defense. Now the lakes were fast receding—and the state of Illinois was begging the Army Corps of Engineers to increase its 88-year-old diversion of Lake Michigan water into the Mississippi River system. Protected by a U.S. Supreme Court decree at the level of 3,200 cubic feet per second, Chicago was then the only significant physical diversion of Great Lakes water out of the system.

The problem of Illinois and other states just to the west of the Great Lakes was that they, too, were struggling with a drought. It was severe enough to strand barges on the Mississippi River. "A giant bottleneck of barges began to build in the Mississippi River Wednesday as record low water levels forced the Coast Guard to close the waterway to commercial traffic," reported the *Chicago Tribune*, noting that barges had run aground near Sainte Genevieve, Missouri and in the Ohio River near Mound City, Illinois.[1]

With no certainty as to when rain would fall again, Governor Jim Thompson was requesting a temporary tripling of the allowable amount

15

removed from Lake Michigan to flush Chicago's sewage and float barges along a canal system linked to the Illinois River. He was serious, too. Don Vonnahme, a spokesperson for the Illinois Department of Transportation, said the increased diversion was justified because so much more commerce floated up and down the Mississippi than across the Great Lakes.[2] Although other Great Lakes states insisted that regional consultation on the proposal was required, Vonnahme said, "We feel that in the national interest, the Corps can just go ahead and do this." He urged the Army Corps of Engineers to use its emergency powers, which authorize it to improve navigation, to support the diversion.[3]

In Michigan the response was emphatically negative. The *Detroit Free Press* called Thompson's pitch "a bad idea—environmentally, economically and politically. . . . Free-lance initiatives by politicians seeking parochial advantage won't enhance [the] process. The very abundance of the Great Lakes as the world's largest source of fresh water—and an integral asset of the region's economy—argues more for their protection than their exploitation."[4] Elizabeth Harris, in a letter to the editor of the same newspaper on behalf of the East Michigan Environmental Action Council, lauded my boss for "calling upon the other Great Lakes governors to honor their commitment to protect the vital water resources of the region."

Word on the street was consistent with that. "Don't let 'em take our water," Governor Blanchard reported hearing from spectators and handshakers on his wanderings. When he assured them that he wouldn't allow it, they beamed at him and gave at least the equivalent of a thumbs-up. "It's a great issue. It's on everyone's mind," he observed.

The summer of 1988 was also the summer in which millions of Americans first heard the term *greenhouse effect*. In controversial testimony before the U.S. Congress on June 23, National Oceanic and Atmospheric Administration scientist James Hansen said memorably, "It is time to stop waffling and say that the evidence is pretty strong that the greenhouse effect is here." Suddenly, public attention was riveted on the media-exaggerated image of a parched, sweltering planet. Added to the natural inclination of Michiganians, this was enough to stiffen resolve against tapping Lake Michigan to benefit Illinois and Mississippi river barges. I participated in several indecisive conference calls during which representatives of seven states and two provinces incredulously quizzed Illinois officials about their preliminary request for a large increase in the biggest existing out-of-basin Great Lakes diversion.

Fortunately, Governor Thompson of Illinois hesitated in the face of unanimous resistance, and then the rains came. The barges floated again without an increase in the diversion. But it had been pretty close. We'd been talking in 1985 about protecting the Great Lakes from Sunbelt bandits. But the first serious threat of an increased export of Great Lakes water had come from a Great Lakes state.

So would the second, the third, and the fourth.

In 1987, Pleasant Prairie, Wisconsin, a community just outside the Great Lakes Basin, had asked for about 250,000 gallons per day of Lake Michigan water to replace its radium-contaminated drinking-water supply. The application, submitted by Wisconsin governor Tommy Thompson to the other seven Great Lakes governors, bounced around for a couple of years. In Michigan, particularly, the issue was politically ticklish. The amount of water seemed small and the public need compelling. But what would the voters of Michigan think in 1990, when Governor Blanchard was up for reelection, if he became the first chief executive in the state's history to sign off on a diversion of Great Lakes water? Was there a way to say yes without saying yes?

By the time Michigan made up its mind, I was no longer working directly for the governor of Michigan. I'd taken a new assignment in a separate state agency. But shrewd minds in the Department of Natural Resources had figured out a way to maintain neighborly relations with Wisconsin without putting Governor Blanchard on record.

In a December 12, 1989, letter, the Michigan DNR director, David Hales, replied for the state. Admitting that any diversion of Great Lakes water was "extremely sensitive," Hales said the proposed Pleasant Prairie diversion was "not unreasonable." Michigan would not object in part because it understood the diversion to be "temporary" and due to end by approximately 2010. But Hales also said that, because the amount of water proposed to be diverted was no more than 3.2 million gallons per day (up from the original 250,000), less than the 5 million gallons per day threshold set for regional review in the 1985 Great Lakes Charter, Michigan had "no formal role in your decision."

What Michigan *didn't* address was something called WRDA, which stands for the Water Resources Development Act. Under section 1109 of

WRDA, which became law in late 1986 and provided the teeth the Great Lakes Charter lacked, the law's most important provision was so direct and clear that it is worth quoting here.

> No water shall be diverted from any portion of the Great Lakes within the United States, or from any tributary within the United States of any of the Great Lakes, for use outside the Great Lake basin unless such diversion is approved by the Governor of each of the Great Lakes States.[5]

Called informally a "veto clause," the section 1109(d) language was actually tougher than that. It required all eight governors of the Great Lakes states to *approve* any new diversion of Great Lakes water before it could proceed. Silence by a single governor, then, would presumably stop a proposal. In other words, contrary to the Michigan DNR letter to Wisconsin governor Thompson, Michigan's governor clearly did have a formal role in the Pleasant Prairie decision had he chosen to exercise it. But Governor Blanchard said neither aye nor nay to the Pleasant Prairie diversion, and it went ahead.[6]

In 1992, Lowell, Indiana, also just outside the basin, asked under WRDA for 1.2 million gallons per day of Lake Michigan water to replace its fluoride-tainted drinking-water supply and didn't get it when Michigan governor John Engler vetoed the request. Engler said Lowell had not considered prudent alternatives and wanted to avoid the higher cost of them while taking Lake Michigan water to promote growth rather than simply meeting current needs. In 2004, Lowell more or less admitted the point while continuing to grouse about the unfairness of Engler's veto. "Town officials say the present wells are adequate, but lake water would allow Lowell to grow at the faster rate of suburbs to the north," reported the *Northwest Indiana Times*.[7]

No fan of Engler, I indulged in one of the cheapest shots I've ever taken at a politician when, in 1994, a source in Michigan's DNR slipped the word to me that new measuring systems had revealed that Chicago was taking more Lake Michigan water than had been authorized by the Supreme Court (I was now an employee of Clean Water Action, a national environmental lobby with offices in Michigan). Engler was up for reelection and at the time was considered vulnerable. He could be characterized as asleep at the wheel while Chicago and Illinois lowered Lake Michigan, I believed, even though excess water had left the lake under several of his predecessors, too. This could be the subject of a first-rate campaign ad by his opponent. An op-ed piece I authored for the *Detroit Free Press* made the tenuous case against Engler and resulted in an immediate and furious counterattack by his people. In the end, the Great Lakes states negotiated a new deal under which Illinois would slowly "pay back" the extra water, and Engler suffered no political damage. My op-ed column made as much difference in the campaign as a pebble hurled from a beach out into Lake Michigan. I learned, however, that it doesn't feel good to distort a complicated issue no matter what the cause.

In 1998, Akron, Ohio, asked under WRDA for up to five million gallons per day of Lake Erie water to supply its growing south side and received the blessing of Great Lakes governors when it promised to return an equal amount of Ohio River Basin water, thus resulting in what the technocrats call a "no net loss diversion."

What was going on with these proposals for water diversions? A political dance, that's what.

Wanting to save its ammunition to meet a major attack on the Great Lakes, and well aware of its position as the Great Lakes state with the least ability to manage water use within its borders, Michigan was trying not to seem too bellicose to its neighbors. The 1992 veto by Governor Engler—the only one under the act up to that time—came not far into his first term when his grip on office was not secure. By the time Akron lined up for Lake Erie water in 1998, he was about to secure his third term by a wide margin and didn't need to worry about accusations that he was soft on Great Lakes draining.[8] By then it was more important that his fellow Great Lakes governors consider him a reasonable man, not one reflexively opposed to all new diversions from the Great Lakes.

It also helped that Akron officials were wise enough to retain a prominent consulting firm based in Lansing, Michigan, to assist them with making the case to Engler and his aides that Akron deserved its no net loss diversion. The same firm, Public Sector Consultants, would later have a similar impact on Engler's successor in another Great Lakes controversy. But at the time few in Michigan noticed or heeded Engler's approval of the Akron project.

And then along came the Nova Group.

In May 1998, it suddenly became known through media reports that the Ontario Ministry of Natural Resources had granted a permit to a private firm, the Nova Group, which wanted to ship up to 50 tanker vessels of Lake Superior water each year to unidentified private customers in Asia (an amount roughly equal to the annual amount that Pleasant Prairie, Wisconsin, was now allowed to divert). Outraging the public and editorial writers, the proposal was also creative: no one had thought to include "exports" of Great Lakes water in the 1985 charter and 1986 WRDA. Lakes defenders had assumed that aqueducts and pipelines, not vessels, would be the route of choice for water takers.

Turning Great Lakes water into a product—especially the water of Lake Superior, the purest and coldest of the lakes—fueled indignation on both sides of the international border. The Nova Group gave up its permit, and Lake Superior was given a reprieve. But now there was a new hole to plug in the levee defending the Great Lakes. It was time to get the governors and premiers of Ontario and Quebec together.

By 1999, the political and partisan makeup of the Great Lakes governors was dramatically different than it had been in 1985 when the charter was signed. Five Democratic and three Republican governors, mostly moderates, had agreed to the charter. Six Republican, one Democratic, and one Independence Party governor began working in 1999 on a strategy to address the vulnerability revealed by the Nova Group gambit. The 1999 lineup contained no liberals and mostly conservative to moderate Republicans. This time they came up with a new diagnosis of the problem. It would become the dubious inspiration for a case of Great Lakes groupthink.

A generous grant from the Great Lakes Protection Fund, a $100 million endowment established by the more progressive band of governors in 1986 to support scientific research on the Great Lakes, paid twelve water law experts to analyze the strength of the region's defense against water raids.[9] Headed by James Lochhead, a western water law expert with experience litigating over the Colorado River, the resulting report became known as the Lochhead document. Before long, it would become the largely unquestioned wisdom guiding the Great Lakes governors and premiers to a new strategy—even though its analysis is based on arguable assertions about international trade and omitted an examination of eastern riparian law and public trust principles that apply in the Great Lakes region. Here's what it says, in brief.

- *You can't just say no to water diversions and exports.*
  "[T]he ability of any authority—state provincial, federal or bina-
  tional—to impose outright prohibitions on water exports is con-
  strained by U.S. and Canadian constitutional and trade law."
- *Current federal and state law isn't strong enough to restrict harm-
  ful Great Lakes water uses and exports.*
  "[E]xisting authorities are inadequate to the task of comprehensively
  or effectively regulating water withdrawals—and in particular water
  exports."
- *The Great Lakes states and provinces had better come up with a defensible non-discriminatory standard that would permit some water
  diversions and exports but only under carefully-defined conditions.*
  "[H]owever it is adopted, a commonly applied, resource-wide decision making standard that ensures benefit to the waters and water-de-
  pendent resources of the Great Lakes Basin, would most effectively
  promote the goals of conservation and sustainable use."[10]

This three-point observation would soon become the basis for more
than six years of painstaking negotiations among the states and provinces
on the way to a new Great Lakes compact. Unfortunately, each of the three
points was an argument not a fact. It was legal advice not gospel. But in the
Great Lakes region, where a handful of executives, staffers, funders, and
reporters shaped the debate, the difference in impact was negligible.

The most important weakness in the three-point argument is the
first—that "just saying no" won't work. Not all lawyers agreed—especially
those with experience in something known as public trust law. One of these
was Chris A. Shafer, a longtime public trust protector who worked for the
Michigan Department of Environmental Quality (DEQ) and DNR, and
later gained a law degree and began teaching at Cooley Law School in
Lansing.

The Lochhead document, Shafer pointed out, overlooked several relevant cases and considerations. In the 1986 *Maine v. Taylor* decision, the
U.S. Supreme Court upheld an outright ban on the importation of foreign
baitfish due to the risk of disrupting the state's natural resources through
the introduction of a nonnative species and because there was no less discriminatory means of protecting the environment. "By analogy, a ban on
diversions of Great Lakes water could be defended on the basis that it is

needed to protect the Great Lakes ecology, especially fisheries and wetland habitat, and that there is no less discriminatory method available," argued Shafer.[11] One implication of Shafer's argument is that the fragility of the Great Lakes system makes it vulnerable to unforeseen disruptions in the event of major new consumptive uses and diversions.

In another paper, Shafer observed, "The lesson seems clear from *Taylor* that with the proper scientific and ecological justification, stringent state regulations, up to and including bans on certain activities, will be upheld provided the state applies the regulation in an evenhanded manner and less intrusive measures are not reasonably available."[12]

Shafer went on to acknowledge that the argument advanced in *Maine v. Taylor* may not by itself be sufficient to withstand a concerted interstate commerce challenge, "but the report should in fairness advise the governors of all reasonable legal arguments, and not paint the situation in the most negative possible light." That the report did not do so was a disservice. By foreclosing discussion of the *Taylor* ruling, the Lochhead study shaped debate toward the apparent desired end of the authors—to produce a water regulatory regime similar to that found in states governed by the prior appropriation doctrine, a feature of western not Great Lakes water law.

The Lochhead analysis rested heavily on three Supreme Court cases that concerned groundwater, not surface water. There are significant differences in the legal treatment of these resources. The nature of groundwater—which sometimes flows only inches per year and lies beneath the earth's surface like minerals—has lent itself to claims of private ownership. It has therefore sometimes been regarded as an article of commerce while surface water, which flows rapidly between and among parcels of privately held land, has not.

The Lochhead analysis did note the Supreme Court's finding in the 1982 *Sporhase* ruling that "there is more to state ownership or regulation of water than there is to state ownership or regulation of other natural resources, because water is essential for human survival and other resources are not."[13] In the court's words, it would be "reluctant to condemn as unreasonable [under the commerce clause] measures taken by a state to conserve and preserve for its own citizens this vital resource in times of shortage."

As Shafer suggested, evidence that water exports or diversions could jeopardize the ecology of the lakes might carry some weight with the courts. Regrettably, however, little research even now has been done to document these effects. A technical workshop hosted by the U.S. Army Corps of Engineers in 1999 was the most recent effort to summarize what is known and what remains to be learned about such effects. The workshop participants concluded that four of ten Great Lakes physical habitats evaluated would likely be significantly affected by a lowering of water level such as that triggered by diversions or exports. But they also concluded, "The magnitude of habitat loss or gain cannot be determined without more precise information on potential water level reductions and the degree of slope lakeward of the habitats. . . . A quantitative assessment of the effects of lake level changes is presently limited by the qualitative nature of knowledge on biological responses to small scale habitat change."[14] The report recommended considerable new research. It has not been done.

One solution that the Lochhead analysis never explored was a U.S.–Canadian treaty to prohibit Great Lakes water exports. Such a treaty—like the U.S.–Canadian Boundary Waters Treaty of 1909—would become the supreme law of the land and trump domestic law, including the commerce clause and the complicated questions arising from it. The analysis may have neglected this possibility because it would require federal, not state action—but the compact that ultimately grew out of the analysis also requires congressional ratification.

The biggest omission from the Lochhead analysis, however, was its utter neglect of the public trust doctrine. That was an oversight almost as big as the Great Lakes themselves. There are several ways to explain the doctrine, but the most important is to distinguish water *use*, which is legal under centuries of accepted common law descending from the Romans, and private water *ownership* or control, which is illegal.

Ancient Roman law divided properties into public and private categories. Within the public categories were the air, the waters of natural streams, the sea, and the seabed. Following the Norman conquest, English common law adopted much Roman civil law, though with modifications. In British law, title to public lands was held in trust by the king for the benefit of the nation. While the king could grant land under English waters, such as navigable waters and tidelands, to private owners, such grants were subject to the public's paramount right to the use of the waters. The king could neither diminish nor destroy that right. Any grant that interfered with the implied reservation of the public right or harmed the public interest was rendered void. Parliament could, however, exercise its policing powers to enlarge or restrict public rights in order to advance a public purpose.

British courts reasoned that the common right to use the sea and navigable rivers was important to commerce and trade and that private appropriation of the use could impair such public benefits. They permitted state regulation of the public use of navigable waters only for public purposes that were in the public interest and only consistent with the preservation of a public right.

The common law of England became the foundation of the law of the original 13 American colonies and, subject to modifications by Congress and the states, of the law of the United States. Courts have interpreted this to mean that the 13 colonies and the original 13 confederated states held sovereign control over their seashores. These states determined the extent of their own public trust shore lands through statutes or the courts. But several core principles were identified and passed on to the 37 states that have since joined the Union. These principles hold that each state:

- Has public trust interests, rights, and responsibilities in its navigable waters, lands beneath those waters, and the living resources therein
- Has the authority to define the boundary limits of the lands and waters held in public trust
- Has the authority to recognize and convey private proprietary rights in its trust lands with the corollary responsibility not to substantially impair the public's use and enjoyment of the remaining trust resources
- Has a trustee's duty and responsibility to preserve and assure the public's ability to fully use and enjoy public trust lands and waters for certain trust uses, including a requirement that the use (whether public or private) promotes a primarily public purpose
- Does not have the power to abdicate its role as trustee of the public's rights in trust resources

As articulated by the U.S. Supreme Court in a famous 1892 case, "the basic common law principle of the public trust doctrine is that the trust can never be surrendered, alienated, or abrogated. It seems to be a rule, beyond question, that the rights of the public are impressed upon all navigable waters, *and other natural resources which achieve a like public importance* [emphasis added]. And the state may not, by grant or otherwise, surrender such public right any more than it can abdicate the police power or other essential powers of government."[15]

As one scholar put it, the public trust doctrine

> is potentially powerful. It can override statutes when they conflict with public trust purposes. The doctrine can provide relief for the decision-maker; it has been crafted by decision-makers. It changes the regulators' job from (a) deciding when should we alter and in many cases destroy natural resources—perhaps gradually but inevitably and with certainty—into (b) drawing a fairly firm line as to which resources we must protect. That is at the heart of the doctrine: identifying what resources should be protected over a period of time that spans generations.[16]

In light of our evolving understanding of the complexity of ecosystems, there is a strong basis for articulating a public ownership interest in natural resources and ecosystems such as the Great Lakes. As another scholar observes, "The characteristics of dynamic ecosystems complicate the task of safeguarding ecological viability. Decision making authority must be vested in an entity with a frame of reference broader, both spatially and temporally, than may be common among private actors."[17]

As Shafer, the former Michigan natural resource manager, argues, the public trust doctrine "provides a powerful means for one or more Great Lakes states to enjoin a diversion of Great Lakes waters that would adversely affect public trust resources."[18] Quoting the Michigan Supreme Court in a landmark public trust case, *Collins v. Gerhardt*,[19] he notes that the rights of citizens to fish, swim, boat and enjoy public trust waters "are protected by a *high, solemn* and *perpetual* trust, which it is the duty of the state to forever maintain."

The Great Lakes Compact signed by the governors of the Great Lakes states in late 2005 declares that the waters of the basin "are public resources held in trust." However, the basic standard used to determine whether an exemption to the ban on diversions or an export or use of water should be allowed is completely devoid of the public trust doctrine. As pointed out by attorney James Olson, "[T]he problem lies in the fact that the public trust standards have not been incorporated into the decision-making standard of the Compact. . . . The lack of explicit public trust standards in the Compact creates a significant dilemma, since . . . the private commercialization or diversion of public trust water in many instances would violate the public trust doctrine."[20]

In other words, a whole body of law reaching back centuries suggests that the Great Lakes states, at least, can "just say no" to water exports and diversions even in the face of the "constitutional and trade law" that the Lochhead analysis claims bars such a strategy. They could do so on the grounds that the diversion or export of water in question would be primarily for private gain or a private purpose, and not a public one, as required by the body of public trust case law. They could do so on the grounds of potentially significant damage to the public trust based on the unknown dynamics of an ecosystem whose character even today outruns the understanding of sophisticated science. Could there be a more "solemn and perpetual trust" than a system of lakes and tributaries containing 18 percent of the world's surface freshwater? The majority of citizens of the Great Lakes states would probably think not. But the Great Lakes governors looked at things differently from 1999 on thanks to Lochhead. It may yet prove the biggest mistake in the history of the eight states if steps are not soon taken to recognize the body of law known as the public trust doctrine.

"I think it's a resource that we have that's certainly a marketable prod-uct," Wheeler said. "A lot of those oil-field boys could kind of cross over. Instead of pumping oil, pump water."

—*Traverse City Record-Eagle,* March 9, 2007

CHAPTER 3

Bottles Instead of Aqueducts

STANDING BESIDE NIAGARA FALLS on June 18, 2001, representatives of the Great Lakes states and provinces solemnly declared their intent to fashion a new pact making Great Lakes diversions more difficult. A pact called the Great Lakes Charter Annex 2001 committed them to developing a regional decision-making mechanism to control the Great Lakes water faucet. Three years after the Nova Group had threatened to ship 50 tanker vessels of water from Lake Superior to Asia annually for commercial sale, the Great Lakes region was resolved to head off water raids.

But 2001 was a significant turning point in the history of the Great Lakes for other reasons.

In March 2001 the village of Webster, New York, advertised in the *New York Times* its willingness to sell "crystal clear well water." Michigan governor John Engler dispatched a letter to the village mayor, reminding him of the 1986 U.S. federal law, the Water Resources Development Act (nicknamed WRDA), which required approval of all eight Great Lakes governors for new or increased diversions of Great Lakes water. "Even though the water in question is groundwater, it appears to be hydraulically connected to Lake Ontario," Engler wrote. "If this proves to be the case, then the diversion or export of this water out of the basin will require the approval of each governor from the eight Great Lakes states." The village dropped its sales offer.

In May 2001 the Perrier Group of America, one of the most famous water bottlers of the age, folded its tent on a proposed million-square-foot bottling plant in New Haven, Wisconsin, in the face of overwhelming local opposition. Fearing that the pumping of springwater by the company would lower the local water table, dry up neighboring wells, and reduce flows in area creeks and rivers, Adams County residents had battled and defeated the giant corporation. The company announced that it had found a more willing state with a similarly generous springwater source: Michigan, the state governed by John Engler. "People were much more receptive in Michigan," said Kim Jeffery, Perrier's chief executive officer. "We're going to have a very successful operation in another state, which will give the people in Wisconsin an opportunity to see who we are. I don't think that enough people did their homework on who we are."[1]

On August 16, 2001, Michigan's Department of Environmental Quality issued permits to the Perrier Group to pump up to 105 million gallons of springwater a year from Mecosta County, bottle it, and sell it in markets beyond the Great Lakes Basin. In succeeding years, the amount of Michigan water the company was allowed to take would grow to 168 million and then nearly 300 million gallons per year.

Not everyone was happy. "There is a great disparity in the way this is working," said an understandably miffed David Galeazzo, Webster's superintendent of public works, in an interview. "On the one hand he tells us if we want to sell water from our system, we have to get approval from governors of all eight states. Now, all of a sudden, the great governor of the state of Michigan is bypassing the procedures. How is the political game played? I'd like to learn it so I can do the same thing."[2]

The superintendent wasn't the only one upset. A group called Michigan Citizens for Water Conservation (MCWC) had been formed when Perrier ▓▓▓▓▓▓▓▓▓▓ by an unlikely firebrand, retired librarian ▓▓▓▓▓▓▓▓▓ a prominent environmental attorney, Jim ▓▓▓▓▓▓▓▓ he springwater wells in a series of adroit legal skirmishes with Perrier and the company that swallowed it up, the Nestlé Corporation.

▓▓▓▓▓▓▓▓▓▓▓▓▓ ions of MCWC was to request a legal opin- ▓▓▓▓▓▓▓▓▓▓ ic attorney general, Jennifer Granholm, on ▓▓▓▓▓▓▓▓▓▓ t of springwater from Michigan to markets ▓▓▓▓▓▓▓▓▓▓ required the approval of all eight Great

Lakes governors, as Republican Engler had said earlier in the year when Webster, New York, advertised its desire to sell groundwater. Rumored to be a candidate to succeed Engler as governor in 2002, Granholm had no reason to make it easy for the incumbent to ignore WRDA. Swier's group ably reasoned that it could obtain a legal opinion on the merits of the act.

In her opinion, delivered on September 13, 2001, to the three Democratic state legislators who had formally requested it, Granholm said that Engler had been right the first time when he confronted the village in New York.

> While the language of the statute [WRDA] may seem straightforward—it prohibits the diversion or export of "water" from "any tributary" of the Great Lakes "for use outside the basin" without the approval of the governor—its terms are broad and undefined. As I analyze the terms, I agree with Governor John Engler, former Attorney General Frank Kelley, and U.S. Senator Carl Levin and other members of Michigan's congressional delegation, all of whom have concluded that groundwater hydrologically connected to the Great Lakes and their tributaries is covered by the protections of this federal law. It is my understanding that the proposal in question, if implemented, will extract groundwater that feeds the Little Muskegon River, a tributary of Lake Michigan. The withdrawal and bottling of such water for sale in interstate commerce outside the Great Lakes basin would constitute a diversion or export "for use outside the basin" and therefore would be subject to the WRDA.[3]

Granholm politely suggested to Engler that he consult with the other Great Lakes governors on the Perrier project, just as Engler had asked Webster, New York, to do, writing,

> There appears to be a lack of consensus among the governors on several critical questions raised by this particular proposal, including the question of whether they deem the extraction of groundwater to be covered by the WRDA and whether they recognize that it applies to the withdrawal and bottling of water for sale in interstate commerce. Consultation in this case would provide the governors with an opportunity to

reach a consensus on these important questions, as the governors and premiers work to develop the decision-making standards called for in the recently signed Annex to the Great Lakes Charter.

Granholm added, "Swift opposition by the state of Michigan to [the Webster] proposal sent a clear signal that we are willing to protect Great Lakes water. But that signal must not be interpreted as self-serving, aimed only at proposals to sell Great Lakes water removed from other states."

Engler was having none of his attorney general's advice. "This opinion isn't something the administration asked for," said Matt Resch, an Engler spokesperson. "It doesn't change the governor's view of the situation." In fact, agencies acting under Engler's direction continued to shower approvals on the Perrier project. State and local agencies provided Perrier with over $2.2 million in state education tax abatements, more than $7.1 million in local property tax abatements, $80,000 in new worker training assistance, and $150,000 for site development and public infrastructure.[4]

Undaunted, MCWC continued its lawsuit against Perrier, citing both traditional riparian common law and Michigan's 1970 Environmental Protection Act, even as the plant opened on May 4, 2002. By then, Granholm was an official candidate hoping to succeed Engler as governor and was embroiled in a three-way primary contest for the Democratic nomination. In her bid to defeat Congressman David Bonior and my former boss, ex-governor James Blanchard, Granholm released an environmental platform that included a "Clean Water Forever" initiative. The platform included the flat statement that Granholm would "exercise her authority under federal law to veto any proposed export or transfer of Great Lakes water that is not coupled with measures that improve the ecosystem both locally and as a whole." It sounded good—and unequivocal—unless you read it closely.

In November 2002, Attorney General Granholm became Governor-Elect Granholm with a narrow win over Republican opponent Richard Posthumus. In the summer of 2003, MCWC and Nestlé Waters North America made their arguments to a Mecost Lawrence C. Root. After a few months of susp that delivered everything MCWC had hoped fo ordered the company to stop pumping grou Springs, the headwaters of Dead Stream, within 21 days of November 25, 2003. Significantly, he found:

There are two natural resources that are so transient in nature as to not lend themselves to traditional concepts of ownership: air and water. We all have use rights regarding them, especially air. Water is more confined than air, so rights regarding its use may turn on a number of legal and factual issues. In the exercise of these use rights both air and water can be "captured" and incorporated into commerce in various ways, but the rights to do so are not unlimited since such capture is only a form of temporary use that must be measured against the rights of others to use the same resources.

. . . In cases where there is a groundwater use that is from a water source underground that is shown to have a hydrological connection to a surface water body to which riparian rights attach, the groundwater use is of inferior legal standing than the riparian rights. In such cases, as here, if the groundwater use is off-tract and/or out of the relevant watershed, that use cannot reduce the natural flow to the riparian body.[5]

Significantly, Root distinguished between use of water by riparians and the sale of water as a product by Nestlé. If "water is the product," he wrote, drawing a line between this and other Michigan industries that use water to make something else, such as farming or beverages like beer or carbonated drinks, "I belie   which to limit its removal as water fron   in."

Root's opinion w   ted from a conservative rural judge. Root held that any effort to take groundwater out of a watershed (for commercial sale among other things) is inferior to the rights of riparian landowners to enjoy, benefit from, and use the waters that would be affected by the export. Any groundwater pumping on the scale Nestlé undertook—so it could market "springwater" taken from headwaters zones—would inevitably have an effect on the associated stream. The ruling rejected Nestlé's contention that there was a margin of water in virtually any Michigan stream or lake that could be captured for export and sale.

The MCWC membership was euphoric. According to the group's attorney, Olson, "We got everything we wanted." A few weeks after the ruling, Swier said she was sorry that 120 workers at the nearby Nestlé bottling plant would be laid off. She added in a news release, "It is really a matter between the company and the employees it hired. The Judge warned Nestlé/Ice Mountain twice that it was building and continuing to expand at its own risk, but it chose to forge ahead with the building of the plant and the production of bottled springwater. We would hope that the company informed its employees of this risk when they were hired."[6]

In Michigan environmental circles, the ruling was welcome, though shocking. Few had expected a fledgling green organization with a pauper's budget to challenge and defeat the nearest arm of a giant international corporation. The environmental grass roots had delivered a powerful message to the grass tops. The group's win was monumental and a little embarrassing to all the well-funded organizations that had sat on the sidelines during the previous two years.

The good news to Nestlé foes was that Governor Granholm had clearly affirmed her position both as Michigan's attorney general and as a candidate for its governorship. Great Lakes water would never be sold as the Nova Group had proposed in 1998. And Granholm clearly believed that federal law required, at a minimum, approval by all Great Lakes state governors of any proposed exportation of water from the region whether in bottles, pipelines, or ships. Nestlé was on its own.

Ah, no. Appealing directly and behind closed doors to Granholm and the director of her Department of Environmental Quality, Steven Chester, the company won an astonishing concession: the department would intervene in an appeal of Judge Root's decision *on behalf of the company*. Legal niceties aside, this was a complete about-face. On December 16, 2003, giving special weight to the intervention of the state, the Michigan Court of Appeals stayed Root's order that the Nestlé pumping be stopped and said it would consider the appeal. This time the surprise belonged to MCWC. Swier said, "At a time when the MDEQ and Administration should have jumped in and rolled up their sleeves to help MCWC, it sat on the sidelines while ordinary citizens and their attorneys, without resources other than commitment to what is right, pursued the matter to a positive, sound result, one that the Administration and MDEQ should be proud of, thankful for, and support from here forward. . . . Governor Granholm, the MDEQ and the legislature must be urged to join citizens and help lead, and not join or support the special interests of international food giants who seek only to profit off Michigan's water in exchange for a few jobs."

What happened? As always, there was an official explanation, which contained some truth, and the whole story.

The official version was the text of a news release posted on the DEQ

Web site. In it, Director Chester said, "With its opinion, the [Circuit] court has provided guidance on DEQ's ability to issue permits. The court suggests that DEQ had the statutory ability to issue a permit in this case. By filing this amicus, the state is asking for the time to review those changes and complete the development of a comprehensive standard on groundwater withdrawals." The release added, "Director Chester says Governor Granholm believes that with 20 percent of the world's fresh water supply within our reach, the state has a moral and legal obligation to ensure that we are the best possible stewards of the extraordinary resource."[7]

But even these scripted words had a false ring. For one thing, the release noted that not only Chester but also David Hollister, the director of Michigan's Department of Labor and Economic Growth, had filed the amicus brief to the Court of Appeals requesting a partial and conditional stay of the Mecosta County Circuit Court decision requiring Nestlé Corporation to cease its operations. The mission of Hollister's agency was to protect jobs now, not fret about enacting reasonable groundwater protection legislation. Hollister said as much in the release, which read, "Nestlé Corporation has indicated quite clearly that it will have to lay off approximately 120 workers without pay by January 31, 2004, if they shut down pumping at the Sanctuary Springs. A partial stay will provide the plant workers and families some economic stability while putting in place reasonable protective measures to limit the potential for any significant environmental harm during the appeal process."

The Granholm team, as would prove customary, wanted to have it both ways. It wanted to profess sound stewardship of water while saving any job that might be at risk from standards enacting that stewardship and providing a greater long-term public benefit. Officeholders, after all, are not elected in the long term, and Granholm's reelection bid was less than three years away.

It was even more stark than that. The agency had had no intention of intervening in the Nestlé case until Chester was paid a visit by representatives of the company and William Rustem, vice president of Public Sector Consultants, one of the state capital's most influential quasi-lobbying firms. Before taking office on January 1, 2003, Granholm had offered the respected Rustem the job of directing the Michigan Department of Natural Resources. Although he declined the job, he had remained influential

with the Granholm crowd. He and Public Sector Consultants had been re-
tained by Nestlé/Perrier almost since the company's entry into Michigan.

As the months and years passed, Rustem became increasingly visible as
the spokesperson for Nestlé and other regulated interests. At one public
forum, he dismissed concerns about depletion of water through mining by
commercial interests. "Water is moving in and out of the Great Lakes con-
stantly," he said, implying that what would be taken would be replaced.[8]
On a global basis, he was right; the essentially finite amount of water will
change little. But *where* it is can change as a result of human actions such as
commercial exportation.

Part of the story, then, is that the Granholm administration was listening to a paid consultant for an industry it had once officially urged be
checked under federal law. But there is so much more to the story, and it's
called marketing.

Some critics say that "water shouldn't be privatized because it's a basic human right." But even if one believes that making a profit on water is a bad thing, I don't see how one could reasonably prevent it from happening. As experience has shown, public water and for-profit bottled water each have their place and seem to co-exist more or less peacefully.

—Tom Williams, in *Water Technology* magazine

CHAPTER 4

A Giant Loophole

HOW DO YOU TAKE something to which most people in a given community would object and render it not just seemingly harmless but a positive social good?

One answer to that question is obvious in modern American society: shrewd marketing.

When the Nova Group conjured up the image of giant vessels moving water from Lake Superior to Asia in 1998, it was overlooking that fundamental fact. When Nestlé Waters North America began working on Michigan decision makers and negotiators of a Great Lakes compact, it was heeding the same lesson. Marketing may not be everything, but it sure helps grease the skids.

Even environmental groups have taken to "branding" themselves. Taking a page from the playbooks of often successful commercial interests, professional green groups have sponsored public opinion surveys and focus groups and developed messages based on the research that is designed to "resonate" with the "values" of the public.

It should come as no surprise that a major multinational corporation does the same thing. But what has been instructive in the Nestlé effort is the degree to which the marketing has worked even on environmental advocates themselves.

Marketing water exports in small containers instead of water exports in oceangoing tankers does have inherent advantages. For one thing, although the water will often not come back to the Great Lakes Basin, it exits in millions of 16- or 20-ounce bottles, and that's much harder to visualize.

But that alone wouldn't make bottled water exports seemingly tolerable. It's important to adopt language that resonates with modern American values.

For example, it is no longer acceptable in American law or decent social circles to discriminate against persons on the basis of race, gender, or other factors. Few Americans want to think of themselves as unfairly biased against something on the basis of its classification. Extend that logic to containerized water and you have the first step toward a marketing strategy.

Perhaps the most persuasive—if bogus—marketing tactic is to compare the pumping of water from natural sources and its sale as no different than the pumping of water to make cars, fruit juice, or widgets. In Michigan, Nestlé has recited this mantra so often that it has begun to seem like truth to many. For example, the *Muskegon Chronicle* reported that Nestlé spokeswoman Deb Muchmore, contended, "Nestlé's Ice Mountain operations boost Michigan's economy without harming its environment. . . . [M]any other companies in Michigan—including soft drink firms, juice makers, food producers and golf courses—use more water each year than Nestlé."[1]

There are so many things wrong with that statement that it's difficult to know where to begin, but the most amazing trick is that it is not factually inaccurate, just profoundly misleading. Here are three of the most salient points.

- *Soft drink firms, juice makers, food producers, and golf courses aren't selling water.* Only Nestlé Michigan is. In effect, it is claiming ownership of the water it sells. Soft drink firms and food producers are, at least in theory, adding value to the water they use to make commercially valuable products—something that ages of common law define as a legal use of water—without conveying water ownership to these companies.
- *Nestlé is targeting vulnerable areas for its water.* Golf courses and fruit juice makers don't seek out springs at or close to the source of cold-water trout streams for a source. They generally decide where to lo-

cate and then seek out an available source. But Nestlé Michigan is unashamedly selling "springwater"—which by federal regulation must come from a groundwater source flowing to a stream, typically at or near its headwaters.

- *Boiled down to basics, Nestlé's argument is that there is typically a "surplus" of water in most streams that is going to waste.* The premise of the commercial water sales industry is that it can take water out of the environment without damaging lakes or streams or any of the associated natural resources such as wetlands, fish, and wildlife. This assumes that not all of the water in the natural flow of a stream is necessary to support its health. In Michigan, Nestlé is targeting multiple streams for its pumping operations, suggesting that each stream can yield a surplus without damage. Even if the assumption is true for an individual stream, at what point does taking surplus water from multiple streams damage the resource into which they all flow—the Great Lakes?

I've had a chance to learn about the industry marketing spin more than once. Sitting in a Duluth hotel room in spring 2005, I was linked via telephone to a Traverse City, Michigan, radio program hosted by Ron Jolly to debate Nestlé spokeswoman Muchmore about the issue of exporting water from the Great Lakes in bottles.

After I outlined the issues with Nestlé's water business and its impact on the Great Lakes, I listened to Muchmore's response. She said, as industry spokespersons would repeat again and again, that water leaving the Great Lakes in bottles was no different than water leaving the Great Lakes in potatoes, automobiles, or soda pop. Water is used in the creation of products all the time and moves across watershed boundaries, she observed. A ban on bottled water exports from the Great Lakes would discriminate, she said. Perhaps even worse, it would amount to the "government picking winners and losers." In that spring of 2005, just after the reelection of George W. Bush on an ostensibly conservative platform, that second phrase must have seemed particularly apt—strong government domestic regulation did not seem popular.

Muchmore said placing limits on bottled water leaving the Great Lakes would choose one class of water export for unfair treatment. Taken to its logical extreme, she said, the state would have to ban, or at least require government permits for, every potato, automobile, or can of soda pop leaving Michigan, shutting down an already troubled economy.

Then it was time for a commercial break. And I experienced perhaps the greatest example of cognitive dissonance I've endured in the entire debate. The commercial was for a children's book called *The Day the Great Lakes Drained Away*.[2] Published by Mackinac Island Press out of Traverse City, the book was touted in the commercial as a vivid way of teaching children about the amazing Great Lakes and the need for water conservation. Perhaps I wasn't quick enough on my feet as I don't recall citing the commercial itself in the rest of the debate.

Later I would visit the publisher's Web page and read the promotional text: "What would happen if we didn't have the Great Lakes? What would we find on our lake floors? These and many other questions are explored in this intriguing children's book. With concern about the Great Lakes paramount, Charles Ferguson Barker set out to create a book that takes children on an incredible journey, revealing the secrets of the lake floors if the unimaginable happened: the Great Lakes drained away. This book serves to entertain, but also to educate—children and adults will learn about the amazing newly discovered geologic features under the Great Lakes. Most importantly, the book will remind readers to never take the Great Lakes for granted."[3] Endorsing the book in a foreword: Michigan governor Jennifer M. Granholm.

With the commercial break done, the debate resumed. I hammered on the threat of commercializing water that belongs to the public. Muchmore stayed on message, repeating her assertions that the campaign against bottled water was not only discriminatory but "emotional"—implying, at least, that it was irrational.

I was naive. I assumed that Muchmore's argument would collapse on its face. But host Ron Jolly seemed to agree with her logic. That's when I realized the marketing of Nestlé opponents was, at least temporarily, losing to the company's more adroit case presentation. But before long I knew I was in real trouble, for many environmental advocates with whom I'd worked for years, and respected for their deep personal commitment to the protection of the biosphere, also wondered why a handful of people were making such noise about bottled water.

These advocates were as close as the halls of the State Capitol in Lans-

ing and as far away as the hometown of Great Lakes United, then the leading Great Lakes citizens lobby, in Buffalo, New York. Increasingly, those
fighting commercial water exploiters such as Nestlé also found themselves
struggling to persuade their friends in Lansing, Buffalo, and elsewhere that
their campaign was worth joining.

In the months leading up to the signing of the Great Lakes–St.
Lawrence River Basin Water Resources Compact and a related agreement
by governors and premiers in December 2005, leading environmental
groups, anxious that the proposed pact might fall through, bargained away
strict controls on the exportation of water in containers. The May 2005
draft of the compact defined water diversion simply as "a transfer of water
from the Basin into another watershed, or from the watershed of one of the
Great Lakes into another."[4] But the October 9, 2005, draft negotiated by
the National Wildlife Federation (NWF) and the Council of Great Lakes
Industries (CGLI), whose language largely shaped the definition in the
final agreement three months later, complicated things by defining water
diversion as

> a transfer of water from the Basin into another watershed. Water with-
> drawn from the Basin which is not incorporated into a Product pro-
> duced or packaged in the Basin and which is transferred out of the Basin
> in bulk by canal, pipeline or new or modified channel, or by tanker ship,
> tanker truck, rail tanker or similar vessel, shall be considered a diver-
> sion.[5]

The new definition left open the door to transfers of water from the
basin as long as they did not occur "in bulk by canal, pipeline," or the other
means defined. And the compromise defined *product* to include "food within
the meaning of the Federal Food Drug and Cosmetic Act." As NWF explained in a memo to other environmental groups, "Therefore, NWF-
CGLI proposal does not define bottled water as a diversion. However, the
proposal explicitly affirms jurisdictional authority to pass more stringent
protections, such as banning bottled water exports."[6] The open question
was whether the states would regard the language of the compact pertain-
ing to bottled water as a floor—permitting higher state standards—or an
absolute ceiling. The other question—apparently not considered significant
at the time by the green negotiators—was whether *any* state could be effec-

tive in preventing exports in bottles, if even one authorized it, especially considering the implications of international trade agreements.

When the governors began signing the compact in December 2005, the definition of *diversion* had again been tweaked to read:

> Diversion means a transfer of water from the Basin into another watershed, or from the watershed of any one of the Great Lakes into another by any means of transfer, including but not limited to a pipeline, canal, tunnel, aqueduct, channel, modification of the direction of a watercourse, a tanker ship, tanker truck, or rail tanker but does not apply to water that is used in the Basin or a Great Lake watershed to manufacture or produce a product that is then transferred out of the Basin or watershed.[7]

The language "any means of transfer, including but not limited to" pipelines and other devices might have brought bottled water back under the compact's general ban on new diversions except for two sentences several pages farther along.

> A proposal to Withdraw Water and remove it from the Basin in any container greater than 5.7 gallons shall be treated under this Compact in the same manner as a proposal for a Diversion. *Each Party shall have the discretion, within its jurisdiction, to determine the treatment of Proposals to Withdraw Water and to remove it from the Basin in any container of 5.7 gallons or less* [emphasis added].[8]

Where did the magic number 5.7 come from? No one could say for sure. But because 5.7 gallons equals 20 liters, and liters are a unit of measurement used in Canada, it made sense to look north of the border. A federal statute there, passed in the wake of the 1998 Nova Group controversy, had sought to stem the threat of "bulk exports" from boundary waters such as the Great Lakes. The statute defined *bulk export* to include "any means of diversion, including by pipeline, canal, tunnel, aqueduct or channel." Regulations promulgated under the act added, "The removal of boundary waters in bulk does not include taking a manufactured product that contains water, including water and other beverages in bottles or packages, outside a water basin."[9] So the genesis of the compact provision was a

Canadian law specifically exempting bottled water from export restrictions and defining water in a bottle as a "manufactured product." No one could or would say whether representatives of the bottled water (alias water commercialization) industry had been at the bargaining table, but their influence was apparent.

Speaking for the citizens group that had challenged and defeated Nestlé in a Michigan court, attorney Jim Olson said, "Clearly, the savings clause does not reserve the right of states to determine whether the water should be authorized or licensed in the first place. Once it's a product, it will be very difficult to turn back the clock to regulate or control it in the future."[10] Speaking of both the proposed compact and a twin agreement between the states and the provinces of Ontario and Quebec, Michigan Citizens for Water Conservation cofounder Terry Swier added, "These two agreements may save the Annex process that so many have worked hard for, but they will not save the Great Lakes. There is a hole in these pacts, and over time the agreements could sink under the national and global demands for our Great Lakes water." Two citizens who had successfully battled Nestlé in Wisconsin, Hiroshi and Arlene Kanno, wrote that state's governor to say, "Lobbyists for Nestlé, Coke and Pepsi have successfully inserted the 5.7 gallon provision to protect their multi-million dollar enterprise. If you allow this provision to remain unchanged in the compact, spring waters throughout the watershed would be fair game."[11]

But other environmental advocates were not overly concerned. Noah Hall, a Wayne State University law professor who had played a significant role in shaping the compact, said the agreement could actually strengthen the Great Lakes region's ability to stop massive water exports by focusing on the natural resource impacts of water loss rather than simply banning exports in containers of any size. "We don't know if water is a commodity yet under international law," he said. "But we want to make sure it is protected even if it becomes a commodity. We can prohibit diversion but it needs to be based on science and conservation, and not economic protectionism."[12]

Added Andy Buchsbaum, the executive director of the National Wildlife Federation's Great Lakes office in Ann Arbor, "We need more protections against bottled water exports. That said, it's not the biggest threat to the Great Lakes. Massive, large-scale diversions through pipelines and canals are a much bigger threat."[13] This overlooked two facts: first, a multitude of bottles leaving the basin would ultimately have the same effect as pipelines and canals; and, second, allowing *some* trade in water in bottles could nullify *all* the export bans in the agreement by essentially conceding that water is a commodity.

It was too late for serious deliberation on such matters, however. The pressure to move ahead on the draft agreement was irresistible, especially with an election year dawning for seven of the eight Great Lakes governors. A historic piece of paper—after four years of effort—was more important than an agreement crafted carefully to withstand the strongest challenge water exporters could bring. "Don't let the perfect be the enemy of the good," you could hear the pact's defenders saying.

On December 13, 2005, at a ceremony in Milwaukee, the governors and premiers announced their acceptance of the proposed compact and associated international agreement. The president of Great Lakes United, Derek Stack, hailed the signing: "As the product of five years' negotiation among ten sovereign jurisdictions, the agreements contain a surprising degree of improvement over the currently abysmal state of protections against water diversion and abuse."[14] A fellow Canadian, Susan Howatt, of the nonprofit Council of Canadians, saw it differently, arguing that the pacts would "severely compromise Canada's ability to protect the world's largest body of fresh water from diversions and commercialization."[15]

Would the states go farther? The first out of the block, Michigan, did not. And again the influence of the water commercialization industry was pivotal.

The most ardent opponent of Great Lakes water exports by others since the early 1980s, Michigan had itself failed to enact water conservation laws in the ensuing 20 years. In fact, only thanks to the kindness of its neighboring states did Michigan participate in the regional review of water withdrawals under the 1985 Great Lakes Charter.

Michigan environmental organizations condemned this hypocrisy and demanded action from the state legislature. In the 2003–4 legislative session, business associations successfully lobbied against the new water withdrawal controls. But in late 2005, as the Great Lakes states prepared to sign the compact, pressure mounted on lawmakers to show that they, too, were concerned about protecting the Great Lakes. Suddenly the business associations, however reluctantly, were ready to deal. They would sign off on a change in Michigan's water laws—with some limits. Only a few of the largest water withdrawals would be strictly regulated. And water removed from the Great Lakes in bottles would *not* be considered a diversion. Representing the newly established Michigan Bottled Water Council, lobbyist Andrew Such made that clear. And Republican allies on the key state House of Representatives committee threatened to pass a harsher version of the legislation, with weaker protections, if the environmental negotiators didn't agree to the tradeoff.

Should the green groups accept such a deal—trading away protection for water packaged in bottles in exchange for getting industry's concession that some water withdrawals needed public oversight and control? The question set off a furor behind the scenes.

In the months leading up to action by the Michigan legislature, the environmental groups, under the banner of the "Great Lakes Great Michigan" campaign, had consistently advocated a six-point program for protecting the state's water. One of the six points was:

Prohibit private sale of water without legislative approval. Michigan needs to take control over its water to ensure it continues to be available for Michigan residents and businesses. We should amend the Great Lakes Preservation Act to prohibit the private sale of water unless the project has received legislative approval.[16]

Now that plank was about to be pried loose from the platform. Fearing such a deal, Terry Swier, the head of the citizens group that had been fighting Nestlé in Michigan's courts, said firmly to her green allies, "I am against anything like this." But it went ahead anyway.

The night before a legislative committee approved the compromise redefining water leaving Michigan in bottles less than 5.7 gallons in size as something besides a diversion, e-mail messages flew furiously back and forth within the environmental community. Defending the so-called bottled water loophole, a representative of the Michigan Environmental Council pointed out that in return the legislation provided for public oversight of all withdrawals for bottled water of more than 250,000 gallons per day—versus a minimum withdrawal of 2 million gallons per day for other uses. This "only condones bottled water under some pretty tight restrictions with public input," said a supporter of the bill. "And, I believe (although others will surely disagree) that we would have had worse language if we had walked away."

The 250,000 gallons per day (or approximately 90 million gallons per year) clause had nothing to say, however, about the issue of the private ownership and sale of water—just about any potential "adverse resource impact" on the affected stream or lake. A representative of Clean Water Action complained bitterly: "I am stunned and disappointed in what is unfolding here and urge[d] everyone involved to take a deep breath and think about what is being done in your name. I sincerely hope I am wrong, but I believe the exemption from diversion for the special interest bottling industry will be looked back on one day soon as a turning point for the Great Lakes and the legacy will not be a good one. There is a reason Nestlé wanted the exemption. There is a reason we wanted to prevent it."[17] The day after the compromise bill breezed through the legislature, Michigan Citizens for Water Conservation attorney Jim Olson said in shock, "The legislature lacked spine, and turned its back on what little spine it does have, to enact historic legislation on one of the most crucial benchmarks for Michigan in the 21st century. Money will flow out of here to bank accounts outside of Michigan and other countries, and Michigan will end up like it did after the forests were gone. Water is not as renewable as people think. What should have been received as manna has been received as dollar bills."[18]

Misstating the law's technicalities but generally getting the loophole right, the *Battle Creek Enquirer* editorialized approvingly.

> The compromise agreement also settles one of the thornier issues raised since a controversy erupted several years ago over a water-bottling plant in Mecosta County: Is bottled water a manufactured product or a diversion of water? Under the new laws, containers smaller than 5.7 gallons are considered "products." We think this is reasonable since, as water-bottling companies pointed out, companies that make soda pop or other beverages also use large amounts of water but are not considered to be diverting water from the state if their products are sold elsewhere.[19]

Oh, really? So now soda pop, without which humans had successfully lived for eons, was just like water, the source of life, under Michigan law.

The transformation of water from the public commons to private ownership had just taken another big step.

The origins of bottled water can be traced back to the earliest civilizations. Well aware of water's health benefits, the Romans searched for and developed sources as they set about establishing their empire. According to legend, after crossing the Pyrenees, Hannibal, the famous general of the Carthaginian army, rested his troops and elephants at Les Bouillens in France, the location of the Perrier spring.

—Nestlé Corporation, "The History of Bottled Water"

CHAPTER 5

How Far Can Commercialization Go?

ALTHOUGH IRONIES HAVE proliferated in the debate over whether water leaving the Great Lakes in bottles is somehow less destructive than water leaving the Great Lakes in ocean tankers, perhaps no irony is greater than the claim by Nestlé that bottled water is a consumer convenience dating back to the Roman era. The Romans, after all, bequeathed us the public trust doctrine, which suggests that no private individual can own water. And until recent years that principle seemed untouchable. On the other hand, since the earliest days of the English colonies in the New World, the doctrine has gradually eroded.

John Winthrop, the first governor of Massachusetts, explained the right of the English to take Native American land with this sensitive observation: "[T]hat which is common to all is proper to none. This savage people ruleth over many lands without title or property; for they enclose no ground, neither have they cattle to maintain it, but remove their dwellings as they have occasion, or as they can prevail against their neighbors."

The waste of good land implied in Winthrop's comment, of course, reflects the fundamental difference between the traditions of Europeans and those of Native Americans, to whom "land was home and communally held. People could not alienate the land any more than they could sell air or water. In contrast, individual land ownership conferred wealth and status in European society. Land was a commodity that could indeed be bought and sold."[1]

In the 1960s, trying to help young elementary school students of European descent, like me, understand the Native American view toward land, teachers likened this view toward the approach American society has traditionally taken toward water. "The idea of private ownership of land was as unfamiliar to the Indians as the idea of private ownership of water would be to us," they said, or words to that effect. Little did they know.

What was once unthinkable to late arrivals to the Americas is now increasingly familiar, even comfortable, to us. What's next? Private ownership of air? Oh, come on, you say. But wait.

> Today's on-the-go people enhance their diets with vitamins and natural food supplements. They drink pure water and energy drinks to improve their vitality. So why not enhance the fuel our bodies need most frequently? Enhancing your body's oxygen levels can help sustain your energy level and peak performance and promote increased alertness and physical stamina. So enjoy an experience with Big Ox today and feel the power of OXYGEN.[2]

At 30 inhalations per can, each of which retails for 10 to 15 dollars, that's a lot of power, at least for the "manufacturers." A television station reporting on the debut of this Missouri-based product put it best: "Several years ago, if you heard someone was going to bottle water and make it into a $9 billion industry, you probably would have laughed. Now a company here believes it may have the next product that will have sales growth like bottled water."

That air can be sometimes had only at a price was a shock in the 1980s when formerly free air compressors at American service stations began to carry a charge of 25 to 50 cents. Soon the trendy oxygen bar followed. Now it's canned oxygen at the corner convenience store.

The sudden conversion of the laughable to the commonplace has happened almost as quickly with water in containers. The question is whether that's good for anyone besides the private parties who profit.

In the Great Lakes region, the packaging and sale of water was not an issue until the dawn of the twenty-first century. But small-scale bottling operations in the Great Lakes states are old, dating back to the late 1800s. Artesian waters thought to have health-giving properties were commonly

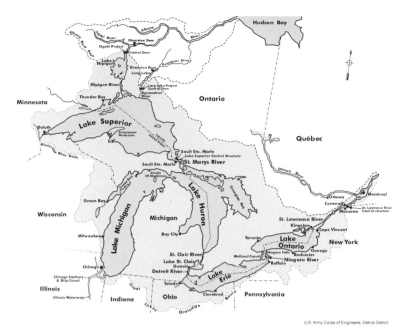

Although eight U.S. states are part of the Great Lakes Basin, only Michigan lies almost entirely in the lakes' watershed, and its citizenry identifies most closely with the Great Lakes. But the state was the last to enact a mandatory water conservation law. Minnesota was the first state to ratify a proposed interstate compact to limit water exports; Illinois became the second state to do so in the summer of 2007. *(Map by U.S. Army Corps of Engineers, Detroit District, courtesy of the Great Lakes Information Network.)*

In much of the Great Lakes region, the popular image of potential water bandits is associated with fast-growing Sunbelt states, as this Michigan billboard attests. But the near-term threats to the waters of the Great Lakes are commercial water interests and communities in the Great Lakes states themselves—but outside of the Great Lakes watershed—that seek water diversions to support their growth. *(Photograph courtesy of Mark Heckman Art.)*

The future of this young Great Lakes beach cruiser will be immeasurably influenced by how Great Lakes communities, states, and provinces, and the U.S. and Canadian governments, manage or mismanage demands for freshwater. The United Nations Environment Programme estimated in 2003 that severe water shortages would affect 4 billion people worldwide by 2050 and that southwestern states such as Arizona will face severe freshwater shortages by 2025. *(Photograph courtesy of the Alliance for the Great Lakes.)*

When water levels are low, the Lake Michigan bottomlands at Michigan's Old Mission Point give a visual clue to what large swaths of Great Lakes coastal areas might look like as global warming and water withdrawals grow in the twenty-first century. *(Photograph courtesy of the National Oceanic and Atmospheric Administration, Great Lakes Environmental Research Laboratory.)*

Wisconsin's Green Bay is one of many historic routes of European exploration via the Great Lakes. In 1634, Jean Nicolet disembarked from a canoe in Green Bay wearing a mandarin's robe, expecting to meet the dignitaries of Cathay instead of the Winnebago people who lived there. The Fox River, which feeds the bay, later became an important portage route as explorers pressed to enter the Mississippi River system. Today the boundary between the Great Lakes and Mississippi River basins is little used as a portage but has become a flashpoint for tensions over which communities should have access to the abundant waters of the lakes. *(Photograph courtesy of Thomas Dempsey.)*

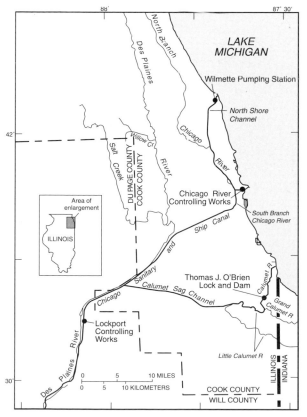

This map illustrates the heavy engineering on the Chicago River that converted it from a natural river flowing into Lake Michigan in the 1800s into a managed river that diverted water into the Mississippi River Basin in the 1900s. The diversion continues. *(Map courtesy of the International Joint Commission.)*

The original and largest direct export of Great Lakes water is the reversal of the Chicago River. Opened in 1900 to flush the city's sewage away from Lake Michigan beaches and drinking-water sources, the Chicago Ship and Sanitary Canal still legally removes 3,200 cubic feet per second from the Great Lakes system. Over 60 percent of the river's diversion away from Lake Michigan is used to supply drinking water for 5.7 million residents of metropolitan Chicago. *(Photograph courtesy of the International Joint Commission.)*

One of the most heavily engineered watersheds in the world, the 156-mile Chicago River is more than a tourist amenity in the heart of the city of Chicago. Its connection with the Mississippi River through a canal also makes it the potential Great Lakes invasion route for Asian carp, which some biologists fear could overwhelm valuable fish species in the lakes. *(Photograph courtesy of Jillian Downey.)*

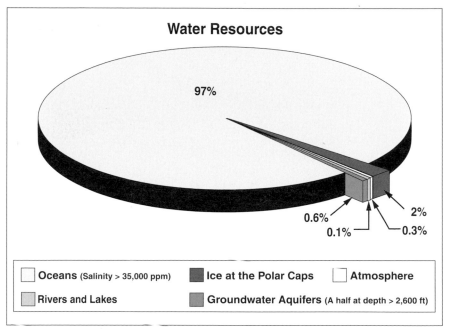

Water Resources

97%

2%

0.6%

0.1%

0.3%

☐ Oceans (Salinity > 35,000 ppm)   ■ Ice at the Polar Caps   ☐ Atmosphere

▨ Rivers and Lakes   ▨ Groundwater Aquifers (A half at depth > 2,600 ft)

Freshwater—the only water humans can drink—is a small fraction of the water on earth. An even smaller portion of the world's water is "available for use" in lakes and streams. *(Data from United Nations Educational, Scientific and Cultural Organization [UNESCO] 1999.)*

Lake Michigan holds 1,180 cubic miles of water and has 22,300 square miles of surface area, making it the sixth-largest freshwater lake in the world. The effects of any one "tap" of Lake Michigan's headwaters might seem insignificant compared to the total volume of the lake, but according to the U.S. Geological Survey groundwater directly and indirectly contributes about 80 percent of the water flowing from the watershed into Lake Michigan. *(Photograph courtesy of Patricia Pennell.)*

In August and September 2007, Lake Superior water levels hit an all-time recorded low for those months, exposing the lake bottom and debris. This is a boat dock on the west side of the High Bridge in the Duluth-Superior Harbor. *(Photograph courtesy of the University of Minnesota Sea Grant Program.)*

Michigan advocates bought newspaper advertising space to pressure legislators to pass the state's first water withdrawal regulations in 2006. The resulting law was controversial on all sides. *(Photograph courtesy of Michigan Environmental Council.)*

OUR GREAT LAKES WAY OF LIFE.
DON'T LET IT GET TAKEN AWAY.

For Michigan, water is a way of life, and the Great Lakes are our most important natural resource. Join the **FIGHT AGAINST PRIVATIZATION** of Michigan's Water. Stop large corporations like mining and water bottling companies from treating the Great Lakes as their own—even **SENDING MICHIGAN'S WATER TO OTHER STATES** and far-off places. Tell our lawmakers in Lansing that weak water laws just won't do. Log on to **WWW.GREATLAKESGREATMICHIGAN.ORG** to see how you can stop the draining of our wells, our waterways and our way of life.

Paid for by the Great Lakes, Great Michigan Coalition. Contact us at www.greatlakesgreatmichigan.org

Despite near-record low water levels, Duluth Superior Harbor at the western end of Lake Superior saw an uptick in commerce in 2007. The low water levels required 22 additional ships to move almost the same tonnage as the previous shipping season. The average lake freighter, which typically transports iron ore or coal, carried 300 fewer tons per voyage than in 2006. *(Photograph courtesy of the University of Minnesota Sea Grant Program.)*

Public opinion on Nestlé's Michigan water-bottling (or water-mining, as critics labeled it) operations was sharply divided. Government officials and some citizens welcomed the company's entry into the state. But angry protests erupted after the company pressed its appeal of a circuit court ruling that temporarily barred it from pumping springwater from western Michigan in 2003. *(Photograph courtesy of Michigan Citizens for Water Conservation.)*

Working without the support of traditional environmental groups, the grassroots Michigan Citizens for Water Conservation used art and bake sales, car washes, and dozens of other community events to help raise over $400,000 to pay legal bills arising from the group's lawsuit against water-bottling giant Nestlé Waters North America. *(Photograph courtesy of Michigan Citizens for Water Conservation.)*

Chris Shafer retired from public service to become a professor at Cooley Law School in Lansing, Michigan. In the summer of 2002, he joined attorney Jim Olson in pressing a Michigan Citizens for Water Conservation lawsuit against Nestlé Waters North America. Shafer and Olson's side prevailed in a landmark ruling—later reversed by an appeals court. *(Photograph courtesy of Chris Shafer.)*

sold. The scale of such operations was miniscule, however, and the idea that it was a threat to a public resource never took hold because most water merchants operated in local markets. A Michigan Department of Environmental Quality list of the state's water packagers showed in 2004 that only the Nestlé operation authorized in 2001 drew substantial amounts of water from the ground for sale to markets outside the Great Lakes Basin. According to Nestlé itself, about 30 percent of the water withdrawn at its Dead Stream pumps in Mecosta County was being sold outside the Great Lakes watershed in 2005.

If the assertion of private ownership of water is not new to the Great Lakes, the exploitation of the asserted right for major financial gain is. Nestlé is not alone in exercising the claim. In the late 1990s, a developer in Livingston County, northwest of Detroit, placed a well on land he had converted to housing and found a marketable resource. In 2002, he offered to sell the water that flowed underneath his land for a cool $2.8 million.[3] Without much blinking, a local public water authority bought him out— apparently not wondering how the developer could own water that didn't belong to him.

He has imitators. An Alanson, Michigan, man proposed in 2006 to take water from wells on his property and sell it as "True Artesian." "The quality of the water, we're just starting to discover, is world class," said longtime real estate broker Doug Houseworth. "All things being fair, I don't think you'll find a better water."

He added: "Finding water that has such well-balanced natural minerals and still tastes good, even at room temperature, is quite rare. It is clean with no after taste. No city-like chlorine, no rotten egg sulfur lingers on the tongue. It is simply refreshing." That's why Houseworth calls True Artesian "good for your body."

It's nothing the nineteenth century didn't see, for even then there were claims about the miracle healing properties of local water sources. What is different now is the potential to take local waters and sell them in bulk quantities on the other side of the planet—for a significant profit. And where there's profit there's likely to be more entrepreneurs willing to take a look.

Underlying the widespread acceptance of and consumer preference for packaged water is a notion that something public is inherently bad and something private is inherently good. For this, in the United States, we have 30 years of conservative attacks on government's competence and legitimacy and a cult of privatization to thank.

"Omnipresent commercial water bottles symbolize more than a convenient hydration source," wrote Saul Landau. "When I buy a bottle of transparent liquid and look at its label, I see a right wing cultural victory, one that will take more than liberal electoral victories to reverse. Will government prove again that it works? Will progressives have energy to re-educate this generation in lessons their grandparents learned during the New Deal?"[4]

Commenting on observations made during a trip to the United States in the summer of 2006, Stephen Hesse wrote in the *Japan Times* that he was used to seeing Americans walking around in public toting cell phones and beverages. "But what caught my eye this time was the bottled-water craze. . . . For years people have been drinking spring water, mineral water and sparkling water, but what used to be a modest health trend has mutated into a worrisome marketing scam."[5]

Like most independent commentators on bottled water, Hesse observed that the price markup for the convenience—anywhere from 240 to 10,000 times—was remarkable. But after interviewing Tony Clarke of the Canadian Polaris Institute, Hesse also expressed concern about the implications of treating water as a commercial product, privately owned. "Selling water, it seems, is not about marketing a value-added product. It is about selling an image—much like a real-estate agent peddling a mirage," Hesse wrote. With so many consumers seduced by the mirage, he added, "the switch is setting the stage for corporations to profit from taking over control of public water supplies."

If so, why should anyone care?

One reason is that commercialized water neither tastes better nor guarantees better health than public tap water. In blind taste tests, consumers generally rate tap water as better flavored. For example, when Corporate Accountability International asked students at the University of Minnesota–Duluth to compare bottled and tap water in April 2006, few were able to do so. Lori Mattson, a junior, walked up to the taste test holding a bottle of Dasani water. "She walked away wondering why she had paid for it," observed reporter John Myers of the *Duluth News Tribune*. "She identified only one of four samples and thought Duluth tap water was

Dasani." She told Myers, "I only drink bottled water because I thought tap water was making me sick. But I couldn't taste much difference."[6]

The key thought might be that tap water is making people sick and thus bottled water is better for them and maybe safer, too. But where does the concern about—or contempt for—municipal tap water come from? And is it based on fact?

Some would say the environmental movement, some politicians, and the commercial news media have demonized tap water, leading to the rise of the commercial bottled water industry. Evidence to support that contention is certainly easy to find. Consider the claims made on one Web site, for example.

"Each day, millions of Americans turn on their taps and get water that exceeds the legal limits for dangerous contaminants."
> —USA Today, Special Report "How Safe Is Your Water?"

"Cancer risk among people drinking chlorinated water is as much as 93% higher than among those whose water does not contain chlorine."
> —U.S. Council Of [sic] Environmental Quality

"Each day in America, about 30 cases of rectal cancer may be associated with THMs (chlorination by products) in drinking water."
> —Natural Resources Defense Council

"U.S. drinking water contains more than 2100 toxic chemicals that can cause cancer."
> —Ralph Nader Research Group

"There's no telling precisely how many Americans get sick each year from drinking bad water. . . . I would say that the cases we learn about are the tip of the iceberg."
> —Deborah Levy; waterborne-disease expert, Centers for Disease Control[7]

Context, however, is everything. Tap water safety in the United States can't be considered without looking at tap water worldwide—or without comparing it to the safety of U.S. bottled water. And, while it is true that environmental advocates have chronically disparaged tap water, with some unintended consequences, they don't deny that U.S. tap water is among the safest in the world. The criticisms these advocates make have more to do with the gaps in protection that remain and whether current safety will be compromised through budget cuts, lack of prevention policies, or the emergence of troubling new contaminants.

So, while the Environmental Working Group, an aggressive nonprofit organization with a penchant for compiling data, can report the discovery of 260 contaminants in 39,000 public drinking-water supplies sampled between 1998 and 2003, it also notes "almost 100 percent compliance with enforceable health standards on the part of the nation's water utilities, showing a clear commitment to comply with safety standards once they are developed. The problem, however, is EPA's [Environmental Protection Agency's] failure to establish enforceable health standards and monitoring requirements for scores of widespread tap water contaminants."[8] The good news, in other words, is that public water suppliers generally comply with safety requirements while the bad news is that the EPA is either unwilling or ill-equipped to produce enforceable safety standards for scores of pollutants. The subtlety of the message may well be lost in the age of the ten-second attention span.

Other environmental organizations are equally or more tough on the safety of packaged water. The Natural Resources Defense Council (NRDC) reported in 1999 on tests it conducted of more than 1,000 bottles of 103 brands of bottled water. "While most of the tested waters were found to be of high quality," it said, "some brands were contaminated: about one-third of the waters tested contained levels of contamination— including synthetic organic chemicals, bacteria, and arsenic—in at least one sample that exceeded allowable limits under either state or bottled water industry standards or guidelines."[9] Even more significant, NRDC reported that safety standards for bottled water were less stringent than those for public tap water. While EPA rules require disinfection to remove bacteria, the Food and Drug Administration (FDA) did not impose the same requirement on bottled water. And EPA requires filtration to remove pathogens while FDA does not. Public tap water operators have to test for organisms such as cryptosporidium, which killed 100 people when it contaminated Milwaukee's water supply in 1993. Bottled water suppliers do not. And, as NRDC pointed out, a significant share of the nation's bottled water comes, in fact, from public tap water, although this is not prominently mentioned on most bottled water labels.

The packaged water industry does not take these truths lying down. "Bottled water is a highly regulated product, subject to federal, state and industry standards," the International Bottled Water Association huffs. In case you don't get the message, IBWA helpfully points out, "Consistent quality and taste are two of the principal differences between bottled water and tap water. While bottled water originates from protected sources (75 percent from underground aquifers and springs), tap water comes mostly from rivers and lakes. Another factor to consider is the distance tap water must travel and what it goes through before it reaches the tap. In compliance with FDA regulations, bottled water is sealed and packaged in sanitary containers. In the unlikely chance a bottled water product is found to be substandard, it can be recalled. Tap water cannot."[10]

What about the 25 percent of bottled water that the IBWA admits comes from the tap? Does the consumer have to be told? Not always, the association admits. If the tap water is subject to "distillation, deionization or reverse osmosis, the bottled water product can be legally defined as purified water, demineralized water, deionized water, distilled water or reverse osmosis drinking water and does not have to state on its label that it is 'from a community water system' or 'from a municipal source.' Processing methods such as reverse osmosis remove most chemical and microbiological contaminants." Most public tap water is processed to remove these as well.

If the negligible difference in safety and taste between tap and bottled water is not enough to persuade consumers to stick with the cheaper public source, it's unlikely that the thought of turning our backs on the idea of water as a public resource will do the trick. In early 2007, a Minneapolis troupe called In the Heart of the Beast Puppet and Mask Theatre publicly announced its commitment to refurbishing and reviving the drinking-water fountain inside its building. "Drinking fountains are modern manifestations of the ancient public wells," wrote artistic director Sandy Spieler. "They are places where people meet in the communal act of sharing water. In addition, our public drinking fountains can teach us of our connection to the source of our water—the Mississippi River—and remind us of the need to preserve its purity and beauty. They also teach us of our connection to all who collectively use the city's water systems, the vast system of workers involved in supplying safe water to the public, and ultimately all who share the finite global water supply." She declared that the theater would no longer sell bottles of water because by doing so "we are unconsciously supporting the marketing of water as an individual commodity rather than assuring the collective right of people to clean water." Multiplied by a thousand, such gestures might at least raise awareness.

The Canadian environmental advocate David Suzuki launched a personal campaign against bottled water in 2007, suggesting that the importation of Evian water from France, for example, is absurd. "I don't believe for a minute that French water is better than Canadian water. I think that we've got to drink the water that comes out of our taps, and if we don't trust it, we ought to be raising hell about that," he said.[11]

As Donald Roy, a Michigan anti-Nestlé activist, observed, "The way for a bottling corporation to stay under the radar and avoid negative PR [public relations] is to claim they are only doing what businesses and municipalities do, namely, use water. Are we going to stop or put limits on farmers, factories, and residences? Of course not. But if and when we have shortages, who will own the water and what will the price be? It is not for nothing that we have public utilities to prevent anti-capitalistic, monopoly practices. Many municipalities in the U.S. and Canada are very worried that this bottled water fad will hurt their credibility as people come to distrust very inexpensive and safe 'public water.'"[12]

Whatever the reasons, more and more Americans are drinking more and more bottled water. The industry reported a 10.7 percent increase in American bottled water consumption in 2005 over the 2004 level. The average American drank 26.1 gallons of bottled water in 2005.[13] An impressed beverage industry association noted that bottled water was now the second leading beverage category after carbonated soft drinks (CSDs), adding:

> The gap between the two top categories is narrowing as bottled water ceaselessly advances and CSDs either barely grow, as had been happening in recent years, or decline, as was the case in 2005. Average intake of bottled water has been growing by at least one gallon annually, thereby more than doubling in a decade. Per capita consumption of CSDs has dipped slightly for several consecutive years. . . . Bottled water's share of the U.S. beverage market is poised to grow, while CSDs' will continue to lose ground.

Growth is a synonym for *good* in American parlance, and the thought of limitless growth is a synonym for "great." Now market economists are wondering why water is not traded as a commodity—implying that it already is one. "Water is about as precious as a commodity can get and it still hasn't been graced with an official trading platform of its own," mused Myra Saefong of Dow Jones Marketwatch in June 2006.[14] Saefong pointed out that only about 1 percent of the water on earth is suitable for consumption and U.S. residents use about 1,000 times more water each day than gasoline. After consulting with market experts, she concluded that, while the economics of long-distance transport of water weren't favorable to creating such a market, supply and demand are on "a decisive collision course" globally, suggesting an increasing value to water in market terms.

Sadly to an entrepreneurial thinker like Saefong, perhaps, no one with vision had yet stepped forward to create the necessary market. "We might first have to have a crisis of some sorts, or a cartel come into being before the world wakes up," she noted, quoting Jon Nadler of Kitco.com.

But there is time before that, at least in the North American Great Lakes region. A little anyway.

GATT [General Agreement on Tariffs and Trade] Article XX
Exceptions:

*"Subject to the requirement that such measures are not . . . arbitrary
or unjustifiable discrimination between countries where the same conditions prevail, or a disguised restriction on international trade, nothing in this Agreement shall prevent . . . measures:*
(b) necessary to protect human, animal or plant life or health . . .
*(g) relating to the conservation of exhaustible natural resources if such
measures are made effective in conjunction with restrictions on domestic production or consumption."*
**Analysts disagree about whether water is exhaustible or renew-
able.**

—Slide from presentation, Forum on Democracy and Trade,
September 2, 2005

CHAPTER 6

When Conservation Is (Trade) Discrimination

SOMETIMES IT'S NOT your adversaries who challenge you the most; it's your allies. Such was the case when Marion Anderson called me up one day in spring 1993 and demanded to know what I was doing to stop the proposed North American Free Trade Agreement (NAFTA). Although I wasn't enthusiastic about NAFTA, I wasn't doing anything professionally to stop it. As the acting Michigan director of a principled grassroots environmental organization called Clean Water Action, I was focused on state and federal water pollution and wetlands protection policy.

But I'd known Marion superficially for almost 15 years. She was well known as the source of numerous studies demonstrating how $1 billion in federal money spent on domestic needs would create a quantifiably larger number of jobs than the same amount spent on missiles. She'd been an early and active supporter of one of my political heroes, Bob Carr, who became East Lansing's member of Congress in 1975 and helped bring an end to the Vietnam War. Hawks detested her, which pleased her all the more.

If you were active in liberal politics in the Lansing area from the 1970s into the first years of the twenty-first century, you couldn't escape her—even though you sometimes wanted to. She possessed the most important and difficult attribute of an advocate—she was relentless. And, although she couldn't have been more than five feet tall and 95 pounds, she was fierce. She walked fast and talked fast. I can still hear her shoe soles slapping on tile floors. Her causes were peace, economic justice, racial and gender equality, and sometimes the environment.[1]

The day she phoned me, her cause was the environment—but not in any way I'd dealt with it before.

"What are you doing to educate people about NAFTA and the Great Lakes?" she said. "Aren't you concerned?"

I told her I knew that fellow green advocates were worried NAFTA would compromise U.S. environmental standards by creating incentives for our employers to take jobs to Mexico, where they could pollute with less restraint. The problems of the *maquiladoras*—factories in northern Mexico designed to attract jobs with lower wage and environmental standards—were beginning to generate headlines.[2]

But I didn't know anything about a problem with the Great Lakes themselves—only about the Great Lakes regional economy, which would send union jobs in the auto industry and related businesses to Mexico. So Marion Anderson educated me.

Although it took me a while to understand her case, its foundation wasn't that complicated: NAFTA, the darling of President Bill Clinton, whom she'd supported in his race for the White House, was going to turn water into a commodity. And the Great Lakes, the largest single freshwater system on the planet, would lose protections against water diversion and become vulnerable to being bought and sold on the open market.

Although foes of the environmental movement think greens are excited anytime they can find another threat to expose, I wasn't excited to be asked to consider the issue. I had enough to do. Paid and unpaid advocates always do. But I also knew that unless I took the time to work with Marion, study the issue, and do something about it she'd never forgive me. I'm glad she called me about NAFTA.

Over the next six months, Marion and I dug into the emerging language of NAFTA. What seemed far-fetched at the outset of our shared labor soon came into focus as a serious possibility: the agreement could legitimize a trade in freshwater. The notion seemed so crazy that most of the reporters to whom we tried to tell the story smirked. Still, in October 1993 I found myself coauthor with Marion of a short report called "Down the NAFTA Drain: Michigan Jobs and Great Lakes Water." In the document we explained how the vague language of the draft NAFTA agreement could convert a publicly possessed natural resource and the essence of life into gold bricks captured and controlled by the mighty and wealthy—and could impoverish Michigan. "NAFTA treats water resources as a 'good' whose export cannot be restricted by a party to the agreement," we wrote. "About 500,000 Michigan jobs are at risk under NAFTA." Quoting a report by the Center for International Environmental Law, we added that NAFTA provided "new hope for developers, agribusiness and policy makers anxious to build a continental water system."

While the White House didn't need to trot out its big guns to discredit us Lilliputians, since it never heard of our report, Michigan's NAFTA supporters, including business associations and conservative politicians, derided our critique as a scare tactic. The proposed agreement had nothing to do with the levels of the Great Lakes, they said.

Still, the negative implications Marion and I and hundreds of other advocates raised in communities across the country did add another straw to a very laden camel's back, and ultimately the Clinton administration did find itself obligated to respond. Clinton's trade representative, Mickey Kantor, and counterparts in Canada and Mexico issued a joint declaration.

> The NAFTA creates no rights to the natural water resources of any Party to the agreement . . . [and] nothing in the NAFTA would oblige any NAFTA party to either exploit its water for commercial use or begin exporting its water in any form. Water in its natural state in lakes, rivers, reservoirs, aquifers, water basins and the like is not a good or product, it is not traded, and therefore is not and never has been subject to the terms of any trade agreement.

To reasonable people, that should have laid the matter to rest. But Marion was never reasonable. She pointed out that the statement was carefully crafted: nothing *obligated* any NAFTA party to exploit or export its water, but that wasn't the primary issue. Did NAFTA open the door to the possibility that private parties would gain rights to take and export water as a product? Marion and others also pointed out that Kantor acknowledged, "When water is traded as a good, all provisions of the agreements governing trade in goods apply." Didn't this mean that proponents of the agreement were having it both ways?

This time, the government did not dignify the argument with a response. Clinton twisted arms and, with the enthusiastic support of the mainstream news media, persuaded Congress narrowly to approve NAFTA.

GREAT LAKES FOR SALE

And so things rested. We all turned our attention to other emerging is-sues and left NAFTA behind. The problem was that it was now the supreme law of the United States. From that platform, it could do a lot to change the way in which Great Lakes water was managed, especially if the public trust doctrine was also forgotten.

Somewhere between the ratification of NAFTA in 1994 and the year 2005, while we were looking the other way—and after Marion Anderson passed away—the prevailing wisdom changed. And even those who chal-lenged the dogma of so-called free trade suggested it was too late to stop NAFTA and related pacts from risking a commercial trade in water. The Uruguay Round of international trade talks, which in 1994 created the World Trade Organization (WTO) to administer GATT and the General Agreement on Trade in Services (GATS), had changed the rules affecting the protection and conservation of water. It had changed almost every-thing, according to the proud WTO.

> It took seven and a half years, almost twice the original schedule. By the end, 125 countries were taking part. It covered almost all trade, from toothbrushes to pleasure boats, from banking to telecommunications, from the genes of wild rice to AIDS treatments.
>
> It was quite simply the largest trade negotiation ever, and most probably the largest negotiation of any kind in history.[3]

According to the WTO, it was also a major advance for world peace.

> The centre-piece and guiding idea of the rules-based system is non-dis-crimination, which arose out of the conviction that exclusionary deals and preferential blocs helped fuel the interwar rivalries, insecurities, and conflicts that drove the international community into another world war. The non-discrimination principle was key to the system's stability in subsequent years.[4]

The WTO also claimed:

> The non-discrimination principle plays an important economic role as well. Non-discrimination is an efficiency principle, both in the sense of ensuring access to low-cost supplies, and of allowing producers to sell in

foreign markets without a policy-imposed disadvantage relative to other suppliers. Similarly, in a non-discriminatory policy environment, consumers can choose freely from among alternative foreign sources of supply. In a world of differentiated, discriminatory trade regimes, doing business across frontiers becomes more complex and time-consuming, implying additional costs for enterprises and impaired competitiveness. For both political and economic reasons, then, the non-discrimination principle has served countries well over the last fifty years, be they large or small, developed or developing.

It sounds reasonable, certainly humanitarian, and almost liberal in some respects. But what does it mean for water and the trade in it?

Section 22.01 of GATT, to which the United States and Canada subscribed at the conclusion of the Uruguay Round, defined as a trade good "waters, including natural or artificial waters and aerated waters, not containing added sugar or other sweetening matter nor flavoring, ice and snow . . . ordinary natural water of all kinds other than sea water." As such, restrictions on the export of said water could only be temporary and applied to both domestic and foreign enterprises. In other words, any prohibition on the export of Great Lakes water put into packages would be vulnerable to a trade challenge.

But what about conservation? Did GATT and its cousins prohibit that? Not exactly. Measures "relating to the conservation of exhaustible natural resources" might be sustained "if such measures are made effective in conjunction with restrictions on domestic production or consumption." But the trick is in defining whether water is exhaustible or renewable. Depending on who you consult, it can be one or the other—or both. Just turn to the Internet.

"Resources such as trees, fish, oxygen, and fresh water are generally considered to be renewable resources as they can be continually reproduced," says an environmental education Web site. "Fresh water from the Earth's recycling process, fresh air from the oxygen produced by plants and trees, and trees and fish which can reproduce themselves."[5] On the other hand, the same site observes, there's such a thing as nonrenewable renewable resources, as "When fresh groundwater gets used up and no rain falls, sometimes for years." That wouldn't apply to the Great Lakes per se, but a permanent lowering of the lakes due to exports might make their renewable waters nonrenewable. Right? You'd have to consult a trade lawyer, not just a hydrologist, to find out.

Meanwhile, GATS, which was also subscribed to by the U.S. and Canada, raises additional questions. It also bars most domestic restrictions on trade and makes no exception for the conservation of resources, renewable or not. And it's unclear whether the provision of bottled water, for example, is a "service" under the pact.

The Forum on Democracy and Trade put it this way.

> Water is a "good," and therefore subject to the GATT trade rules when it is in the stream of commerce. Does that occur when:
>
> • water is in a bottle?
> • water is captured in a man-made structure?
> • water is in the pump or pipeline?
> • A quantity of water remains of an exercised permit?
> • an unexercised permit for water rights has a value and can be sold to anyone on the market?[6]

The questions will not answer themselves. Ultimately only a legal challenge to a restriction on Great Lakes water exports will.

But the questions would have been moot if environmental advocates and their supporters had recognized something that happened between the 1980s and 2005—international trade agreements that substantially changed the rules of the game. In the 1980s, just saying no to diversions and exports was legally questionable under U.S. domestic law. By 2005, when the Great Lakes compact was signed, just saying no on the grounds of conservation was the only way to head off commercial water grabs under international law. Unfortunately, not many environmental advocates were well-versed in trade law.

Another problem emerged after NAFTA while environmental advocates and reporters looked away. The corporate interests that had bankrolled the pro-NAFTA campaign were carefully studying the pact's language, and entrepreneurs were beginning to dream big dreams of everything from towing icebergs to building water-pumping plants to bottling and selling freshwater in the places it is most abundant in North America. Soon they were attracting the attention of reporters again.

In August 2006, the *New York Times* noted that Eugene P. Corrigan Jr., an entrepreneur in Charleston, South Carolina, had "mapped out the logistics for sending empty oil tankers back to the Middle East with their ballast tanks full of excess water. He has yet to get a Middle Eastern country to adopt his idea—'I sense a real reluctance to be dependent on a source beyond their borders for a water supply,' he said—but he continues to try."[7]

Only one giant freshwater ecosystem straddles the U.S.-Canadian border, and is inherently tempting to water marketers due to its size and location. On the northern side of the boundary, the sales magic isn't always alluring. When President George W. Bush in 2001 casually remarked that he was "open to any discussions" about the idea of importing Canadian water, he touched off a furor. In an immediate news release, the nonprofit Council of Canadians complained, "Today's news that U.S. President George W. Bush wants to negotiate a continental water agreement ends any pretence that Canada's water is protected from the thirsty American South-west. . . . Instead of acting decisively to protect our water from nearly five decades of bulk export schemes the Canadian government has spent the last two years trying to reassure Canadians that there is nothing to worry about. . . . Now we know Canadians' concerns were justified."[8]

Exporting Canadian water would be bad for Americans, too, some critics argued. "The ability to control the destiny of one's water resources will be of profound importance this century," wrote Paul Muldoon of the Canadian Environmental Law Center in 2000. "Canada will be faced with vociferous demands for water. The U.S. will continue to eye Canadian water while carrying on inherently unsustainable water practices like farming in deserts. Exporting water to satisfy the unquenchable thirst of the Southwest, especially through some large scale diversion, serves to encourage these unsustainable water uses."[9]

How does this happen? Through trade agreements like NAFTA, says Maude Barlow of the Council of Canadians, for "[as] soon as you take water out of its natural state—bidding on it, trading it for commercial purposes or selling it—it is then a commodity clearly defined under these trade agreements and that's it—you've lost control over it."[10]

Although typically sensitive about the appetite of Americans for their resources, not all Canadians were opposed to selling their lush waters to U.S. markets. "Oil was the focus at the Global Business Forum" held in Banff, Alberta, in September 2006, commentator Diane Francis observed in the *Financial Post*, "but water will become the New Oil. . . . And Canada has an embarrassment of riches, while other nations are sorely disadvantaged. Fresh figures from an expert invited to the conference underscored a very bright future for Canada's water largesse. . . . For instance, one pipeline carrying surplus fresh water from Manitoba to Texas could double provincial and municipal government revenues each year." Blasting "wingnut" politicians of the Canadian Left who oppose selling water across the border, Francis added, "The problem, of course, is pricing. But that will be sorted out [as] soon as parched areas of the United States and the rest of the world begin to attach economic value to the commodity."[11]

What fans of water sales seem to forget is that water is not "renewable" in the standard sense—not like trees, which can be planted in ever-growing numbers. Water is finite. Or, as Canadians Barlow and Clarke pointed out in 2003, "We are taught in school that the Earth has a closed hydrologic system; water is continually being recycled through rain and evaporation and none of it leaves the planet's atmosphere. Not only is there the same amount of water on the Earth today as there was at the creation of the planet, it's the same water. The next time you're walking in the rain, stop and think that some of the water falling on you ran through the blood of dinosaurs or swelled the tears of children who lived thousands of years ago."[12]

To borrow the language of a 1980s economist, water is a zero-sum game. If it leaves the Great Lakes Basin in bottles, tankers or canals, it doesn't come back except for a small percentage in evaporation. So if you start a trade in Great Lakes water—supplying it to those who live outside the basin—you are drawing down the Great Lakes. That's dangerous because throughout the last two centuries the descendants of Europeans have shown that they can inflict damage on the apparently invulnerable Lakes without any intent to do so.

The hydrology of the Great Lakes underscores the seriousness of this loss. As the International Joint Commission (IJC) declared in a 2000 report, "Although the total volume in the lakes is vast, on average less than 1 percent of the waters of the Great Lakes is renewed annually by precipitation, surface water runoff, and inflow from groundwater sources."[13] When 99 percent of the water in a lake system is a one-time deal—in this case, dumped by the glaciers on their most recent retreat—the remaining 1 percent is the measure of its resiliency—and its fragility.

Citing the IJC, of course, has its risks. The final report issued by the same body in response to requests by the U.S. and Canadian governments observed:

> Analysis of the bottled water industry indicates that when intrabasin trade in bottled water is subtracted from the total trade, the Basin imports about 14 times more bottled water than it exports—141 million liters (37 million gallons) in 1998 imported vs. 10 million liters (2.6 million gallons) exported. At this time, bottled water appears to have no effect on water levels in the Great Lakes Basin as a whole, although there could be local effects in and around the withdrawal sites.[14]

Unfortunately, some of my colleagues in the environmental community and their interpreters in the news media took this 1998 snapshot as part of the firmament. If bottled water wasn't a problem for the Great Lakes in 1998, they reasoned, it wouldn't be a problem for a long time if ever.

One might even concede the point if the issue was solely the volume of water exiting the basin in bottles today or tomorrow. But what if the treatment of water as a "good" under NAFTA and other trade pacts means that sending *some* water out of the basin on a commercial basis means that *all* of the basin is up for grabs by entrepreneurs? The immediate local impact is not the issue; the problem is the opened door. Slippery slope thinking, you might respond, in a mixture of metaphors.

Maybe, and maybe not. Listen to this.

> Our Tribes are rooted in and upon this land and these waters of our Great Lakes Region. We have asked our questions. We receive our answers. For generations we have heard the cries and felt the tears of our Mother Earth, felt the pulse of her life blood waters struggling to survive the abuses that have been heaped upon her. One hundred and fifty years ago we had a resource in the Great Lakes region that was considered inexhaustible. It lasted barely two generations. This was the White Pine forest. The White Pine of this century is Water.[15]

As apparently only the tribes now remember, we have lived this experience before. Right here, at home. Natural resources once thought limitless have almost perished within the memories of our grandparents. As a Minnesota physician commented on climate change in 2007, "We humans have a history of underestimating ourselves, and what human civilization can do. Sure, there's a certain humility, a certain anti-hubris that makes global warming skepticism rather attractive. But the track record of *Homo sapiens* suggests otherwise. . . . The daunting, massive expanse of Earth now looks something more like a Petri dish. We deceive ourselves when we suggest that we are powerless to change it, when it's we who have changed it."[16]

How many times must we learn the same lesson? There is a risk that if we don't grasp it soon we may not have another chance to educate ourselves. Perhaps the legal rights held by Native American tribes and Canadian First Nations are the final and best protection. "We're not stakeholders but bona fide owners. The Great Lakes are not for sale," Bob Goulais, a spokesperson for the Union of Ontario Indians, told author Brian McKenna.[17]

The government is being encouraged to take people's property without paying for it. That is flat-out un-American.

—Ohio State senator Timothy Grendell,
opposing the Great Lakes compact

CHAPTER 7

A Compact Only a Lawyer Could Love

THE OLD ADAGE comparing lawmaking and sausage making never seemed more valid than when I sat in a State Office Building committee room in Saint Paul, Minnesota, in the winter of 2007. There I listened to a well-regarded public servant named Kent Lokkesmoe explain the process that led to the signing in 2005 of the Great Lakes–St. Lawrence River Basin Water Resources Compact.

Lokkesmoe, director of the Minnesota Department of Natural Resources Division of Waters, explained to somewhat curious House committee members that the process leading to the compact had begun in 2001 with a determination among the eight Great Lakes states, Ontario, and Quebec to produce an agreement that was "simple, durable and efficient." He added that the agreement was durable and efficient, but it was no longer necessarily simple. After paging through the 26-plus-page compact and supporting documentation, no one on the committee challenged him on the final point.

Signed on June 18, 2001, at Niagara Falls, Ontario, the launching agreement—known as Annex 2001 afterward—was, in fact, simple. It filled four pages only by consuming one of those pages with the signatures of the governors and premiers.[1] The remainder of the text consisted of six directives to the staffs of these chief executives, which included· instructing them, in essence, to come up with a new agreement, listen (or pretend to listen) to the public, develop a new standard for water export decision-

73

making, carry forward the decision-making process under the 1986 Water Resources Development Act (WRDA), use the best available information, and do other miscellaneous things.

But a funny thing happened on the way to implementing these directives. Listening to the public requires giving written assurances in a final document that certain implicit premises and promises are now explicit. That takes room. And listening to special interest lobbies requires far more language clarifying, footnoting, explicating, and sometimes misleading.

A reading of the final text of the compact suggests how it ballooned. Section 4.14, about a page in length, is a legal disclaimer that exempts the 107-year-old Chicago water diversion from the requirements of the compact, thus ensuring the continued use of Lake Michigan water by the city and suburbs. In the original version, it wasn't thought necessary, but lawyers for Chicago and the state of Illinois wanted to be sure.

Another chunk of the compact is pure boilerplate. This caused some problems, beginning in the Minnesota legislative ratification process. Some suspicious state lawmakers fretted about provisions requiring the council established under the compact to adopt an annual budget; who would pay for it? An even more sinister legislative mind-set questioned a clause that referred to "property and assets of the Council," suggesting that the body would become a behemoth intruding on the rights of individuals. The explanation that "property" referred to office furniture and computer equipment did not put this fear to rest.

The first four pages of the compact consist of definitions, and this is not necessarily to its benefit. For example:

> **Diversion** means a Transfer of water from the Basin into another watershed, or from the watershed of one of the Great Lakes into that of another by any means of transfer, including but not limited to pipeline, tunnel, canal, aqueduct, channel, modification of the direction of a water course, a tanker ship, tanker truck, or rail tanker but does not apply to Water that is used in the Basin or in a Great Lake watershed to manufacture or produce a Product that is then transferred out of the Basin or watershed.

Then there's the simple statement on page 15 that "All New or Increased Diversions are prohibited, except as provided for in this Article." But wait. There are two catches.

First, the next two pages are spent defining the "except as provided for." These paragraphs spell out how communities that straddle the Great Lakes Basin divide, and communities in counties that straddle the divide, might be able to take Great Lakes water out of the basin.[2]

Second, the compact provides that the withdrawal of water and its removal from the Great Lakes Basin in containers of 5.7 gallons or less are only a diversion if a particular state decides to treat it as such. In other words, without state legislation explicitly decreeing that the exportation of water in small containers is a diversion subject to the compact's tough restrictions, any amount of water can legally leave the Great Lakes in the aforesaid containers—for now, bottles.

In challenging the environmental advocates who argued that bottled water exports should be treated as diversions just like exports in ships or rail tankers, defenders of the industry said there was no scientific distinction between water used to make grape juice (not regulated) and water alone in bottles. To some, this sounded reasonable. But why? There is no scientific distinction between the impact on an ecosystem of a billion gallons of water removed in containers less than 5.7 gallons in volume and a billion gallons removed in containers *more* than 5.7 gallons in volume. And there is a legal, moral, and spiritual difference between water *used* to make a product, and water *itself* as a product.

But by the time Kent Lokkesmoe was talking to Minnesota legislators, it was too late for all that. The compact would either be ratified, flaws and all, by all eight states, or it would die, perhaps never to be revived. And the foundations that fund Great Lakes environmental groups and the groups themselves could not abide that. In the end, regardless of the merits of the compact, they wanted it ratified. And the sooner the better. That would show the region, the nation, and the continent that after more than 20 years of talk the Great Lakes region was actually passing laws and erecting a legal wall against water exports.

Unfortunately, sausage makers in Ohio and Wisconsin were unable to let the compact pass without swatting at it. They not only had things to say against it but were marshaling active opposition. In doing so, they demonstrated how environmental arguments pale compared to assertions about the sanctity of private property rights. After all, environmental arguments have to do with us all, but private property rights are intensely personal.

In Minnesota, whose legislature easily cleared the compact in February 2007, came early signs of a collision with property rights advocates. In both a state House committee and on the House floor, a stubborn band of conservatives hinted at a dark conspiracy behind the compact. A Republican legislator, Mark Olson, complained in committee that the compact would require a landowner in the northeastern part of the state to get permission from all eight Great Lakes governors to dig a private well for his or her new house. Lokkesmoe's effort to reassure Olson—by pointing out that new withdrawals for drinking water wouldn't be covered by the compact unless they were of a volume to supply a city of roughly 50,000 people—did not do the trick.

In the floor debate Olson was just as passionate. "This bill is so serious. We are yielding jurisdiction of this state over to international courts. I've got so many red flags, I don't know what to do." He added that the bill created a new entity "with power over Minnesotans, but out of Minnesota's control," presumably referring to the "Regional Body" of the states created by the compact.[3] His arguments fell mostly on deaf ears, and his colleagues approved the compact legislation by a vote of 97 to 35.

But over in Ohio the property rights arguments were gaining strength. Led by a Republican state senator from the suburbs of Cleveland, Timothy Grendell, the legislature had nixed an effort to pass the compact late in 2006. "The Compact would convert privately owned lakes, ponds, farm irrigation, drainage ditches, well water, and (potentially) wetlands into public trust property," Grendell argued in a letter to fellow legislators. "This is a major change in property law in Ohio and an unprecedented taking of private property."[4]

What would it mean to a landowner? Grendell had the answer. "You could be told that you no longer have the right to use your well, to exclude other people from your manmade pond, or place a 'no trespassing' sign on your property if it is a wetland."[5] The thought that bureaucrats in some far-removed central office would have designs on individual wells, manmade ponds, and small wetlands would have been ludicrous had Grendell not had enough clout to slow the compact down.

Arguments made by the administration of Republican governor Robert Taft, like Grendell a Republican, were to no avail. "Congress has repeatedly warned Ohio and the other Great Lakes states to deal with this issue here among ourselves—or to have Congress settle it for us," Ohio Department of Natural Resources director Sam Speck wrote to Ohio senators in December 2006. "Congress has the expectation that the states will act. The

Compact is the means by which Ohio and its neighbors intend to meet that expectation. If we fail, then the states must prepare for Congress to act on its own to federalize management of the Great Lakes. Control of this region's most valuable resource will shift from Columbus and the other Great Lakes statehouses to Washington, D.C., an arena increasingly controlled by interests far removed from Ohio's borders."[6]

The specter of a congressional Sunbelt majority turning the spigot on the Great Lakes, increasingly the selling point for compact ratification, was not enough to do the trick. Nor was Speck's interesting assertion that there were "other elements in the Compact that benefit Ohio, and were hard won, for example—how the Compact treats bottled water." He did not explain why Ohio had wanted the freedom to treat exports of water in bottles differently from exports of water in larger containers.

Speck was on target, however, though not persuasive to Grendell, in noting that the compact could not be construed as affecting private property rights without a twist of language. He pointed to section 8.1.4 of the document: "An approval by a Party or the Council under this Compact does not give any property rights, or any exclusive privileges, nor shall it be construed to grant or confer any right, title, easement or interest in, to or over any land belonging to or held in trust by a Party; *neither does it authorize any injury to private property or invasion of private rights, nor infringement of federal, State or local laws or regulations;* nor does it obviate the necessity of obtaining federal assent when necessary"(emphasis added).

Grendell not only succeeded in stopping approval by the Ohio legislature before Taft left office at the end of 2006 but also stalled action during most of the first half of 2007. That in turn set off a tizzy of action among environmental advocates anxious to dismiss Grendell's property rights arguments as nonsense. But all their words could not persuade hostile parties—including the Council of Great Lakes Industries, which had blessed the compact after the bottled water giveaway. The sheer complexity of the compact had become an argument against it for those seeking reasons to kill it, which meant that the same property rights questions being raised by the opponents were being lost in the weeds, even when law and public opinion were clear.

Are lakes, streams, and ponds "waters of the state," protected by the public trust doctrine? Or can a body of water be privately owned and exempt from most or all of government's reach?

More fundamentally, can anyone own water? If a farmer can own a farm pond or a tycoon can own a lake, then why can't Nestlé own part of Lake Michigan? And where does it end?

The irony is that, while Grendell and a handful of other right-wingers were complaining that the compact might steal private property rights, it was more likely that it was going to do the opposite—by *conferring* private property rights, as in trade protections, to commerce in the waters of the Great Lakes.

It might have been best, in the end, if the Great Lakes states had pursued the guidance their governors had given them in 2001 and created a compact that was durable and efficient—and, most important, simple.

Nestlé's ever-expanding water grab undermines the interests of those who live on lakes and streams, the public that fishes, boats, swims, and enjoys our lakes and streams, cities and towns that rely on groundwater and lakes and streams, farmers who rely on our groundwater, and industry and our economy that are so dependent on our water. Nestlé wants to convert water—the source of life—from a public to a private resource. Do we want to turn control of our water to special interests?

—Michigan Citizens for Water Conservation newsletter,
                                                      March 2007

CHAPTER 8

Grassroots Ground Zero: Horsehead Lake

TRAVELING NORTH FROM the Michigan state capital of Lansing, you come close to dozing for scores of miles while crossing a nearly flat, agricultural landscape. An hour later, you see scattered oil and gas wells. The city of Mount Pleasant, which is emphatically not mountainous, welcomes freeway arrivals with a mock oil derrick bearing the city's name. In 2007 it was natural to reflect on the fact as you passed this monument that the state of Michigan imposed far greater levies on the removal of petroleum than on the removal of water from the ground.

Heading west from Mt. Pleasant, the two-lane state highway traverses increasingly interesting terrain. The land waves like a flag in a mild breeze, diving into creek beds and topping small hills. Now and then the glaze of a wetland or small lake off to the side provides comfort. Ultimately, after twists and turns of the main road and a short trip into the backcountry of gravel roads, woodlots, and marshes, you are on a road that winds along the eastern shore of Mecosta County's Horsehead Lake. On most days that I've visited, the lake has been calm or had a slight chop that didn't prevent it from reflecting the benign blue of a mild spring or summer day.

When you park in the driveway of Terry and Gary Swier, the sense of calm persists. The trim but towering Gary and the diminutive Terry are both soft-spoken, gracious, and welcoming, at least to friends. Only the fierceness in Terry's eyes signals the fact that she has been the leading spokesperson for Michigan Citizens for Water Conservation, the underfinanced but untiring legal and political adversary of the Nestlé Company's Michigan water-mining efforts, which began just miles away across Mecosta County.

The battle began in 2001 after Wisconsin opponents ejected what was then the Perrier company from Adams County. When Perrier (later purchased by Nestlé) came to her backyard, she expected it to receive the same treatment. When the administration of Governor John Engler welcomed the company to the state, she was shocked.

Similarly shocking was the "conscience-clearing memo" that an aide to Engler, Dennis Schornack, put on record. In September 2000, when Perrier was seeking tax breaks for its proposed Michigan operation, Schornack told Engler that such incentives could put him in political hot water.

"Because Michigan is in the bottom of the basin bowl, Great Lakes water is defined to include groundwater," he wrote. If the company received state tax breaks, "Michigan won't just be giving away the water; it will be paying a private and foreign-owned firm to take it away."[1]

That wasn't the surprise to Terry Swier; the surprise was that Schornack thought "giving away the water" was good state policy. "Perrier should be thankful that the raw material is free," wrote Schornack, who by the time the memo became public had been nominated by President George W. Bush to be the U.S. chairman of the International Joint Commission, a treaty body that oversees Canadian-U.S. water issues. "If it was trees, natural gas, minerals, oil or even sand, they would compensate the state," he said.

"So he clears his conscience by saying it's fine to give away the water, just don't pay a giant corporation to take it away and make a profit?" asked Terry. "And he doesn't even address the fact that his own boss [Engler] had threatened a village in New York if it did the same thing Michigan was about to do."

Not even the Swiers foresaw, or could believe it, when a community one county to the north of their home not only agreed to sell water to Nestlé but actually sought out the company to do so. Evart, a burg of approximately 1,700 residents, lost a major employer early in the new century. All the water it had once consumed would remain in the ground, generating no revenue for a city that had the capacity to deliver it, reasoned City Manager Roger Elkins. He contacted Nestlé to see whether the company was interested. It was.

In March 2005, the company and the city announced plans to "dedicate" millions of gallons of water each year to Nestlé, which would truck it 40 miles to its Stanwood plant for bottling. In return, Nestlé would build 14 acres of baseball and softball diamonds and a practice football field for the local high school, relocate 300 campsites on the Osceola County fairgrounds—and pay 88 cents for every 1,000 gallons, less than what the company charged at the time for a 20-ounce bottle. Ultimately, Evart would provide 168 million gallons of water per year to Nestlé, more than the 156 million gallons the Nova Group had wanted to take from Lake Superior in 1998, setting off the controversy that had the governors and premiers scurrying to create a Great Lakes compact.

"What's the difference if water's leaving in a tanker going to Asia or if it's leaving in 12-ounce bottles going to Asia?" asked David Holtz, Michigan director of Clean Water Action. "The idea that a company can come in and buy Great Lakes groundwater and ship it out of the basin for sale is a really dangerous precedent."[2]

When Terry Swier and other critics rejected Evart's water-capturing operation, Elkins, the city manager, was mystified. He recalled how the area had been logged in the late 1800s. "The trees were shipped out of here. . . . I don't see water as any different," he said. "We see them as just another customer coming online. You use the water as you see fit."[3] Comparing the exportation of water to the exportation of Michigan's trees a century earlier wasn't comforting to the critics. When the timber industry was finished exporting the trees, most of northern Michigan was a barren, burned wasteland. Only four generations of publicly funded replanting and forest management had restored the landscape.

"Communities that are going to remain viable have to grow," added City Manager Elkins. Grow how much? Nestlé said it planned to hire 50 additional employees for its Mecosta County bottling facility, drawing on the Osceola County labor force.

About 25 percent of plant employees would work in the Evart area. Fifteen drivers also would be required according to a Nestlé spokesperson. In 2007, Nestlé dangled before city officials the prospect of an Evart bottling plant with "200 jobs and millions of dollars in property taxes."[4]

That wasn't all. Nestlé announced in the fall of 2006 that it was seeking approval from the Michigan Department of Environmental Quality to pump 216,000 gallons of water from natural springs feeding Twin and

Chippewa Creeks in Osceola County. The creeks are state-protected trout streams that flow into the Muskegon River. Before public comment was accepted on the proposal, the DEQ, under provisions of the 2006 Michigan water law, announced that the project would not likely cause an adverse impact under Michigan's new water withdrawal law based on data generated by Nestlé.

Late in 2006, Nestlé notified local landowners in Monroe Township, Newaygo County, that it was investigating the possibility of pumping springwater from a site near the headwaters of the White and Pere Marquette Rivers and trucking it 25 miles to the company's bottling facility in Stanwood. At a township meeting in January 2007, over 100 people turned out to angrily protest Nestlé's plan. The White River Partnership, a citizens organization, passed a resolution against the proposal. "If our goal is to help protect the river and the resource, and you look at our group's mission statement, we just felt like we had to do this," said Tom Thompson, chairman of the partnership.[5]

"This is a pristine trout stream. I don't think any water should be taken out of it," river activist Jay Peasley said. Nestlé looked at it differently. "The ecosystems in the White River watershed don't care where the water goes. They only care that there is enough water—do the ecosystems have what they need?" said Gregory Fox, natural resource manager at Nestlé's Stanwood bottling plant. The difficulty, of course, was determining how much water ecosystems "need" and where the "surplus" available for the taking begins.

Nestlé later withdrew the proposal, claiming the waters involved did not meet its exacting standards. But a pattern was coming into view: moving up and down the spine of the northern Lower Peninsula of Michigan, the company was seeking high-quality cold-spring water—the same kind needed to create and sustain trout and other fisheries.

Terry Swier was fighting mad. "What will it take for people to realize what's going on here? Water is water. It's not beer, it's not fruit juice. Nestlé is taking the public's water, diminishing streams and wetlands and telling us we should like it. Drop by drop, the public's water is slipping away."

In classic citizen-activist style, Terry and her 1,900-plus Michigan Citizens for Water Conservation members said they would never give up. In the summer of 2007 they were still holding bake sales, car washes, and poker tournaments—variations of the same down-home fund-raisers that had once bankrolled an astonishing $400,000 legal battle against a giant corporation.

I drove away from Horsehead Lake glad that Terry was on the side of the water.

At a public meeting organized by the local League of Women Voters in the city of Holland, Michigan, in April 2007, one questioner asked panelists whether there weren't political problems with "denying people from other parts of the country access" to Great Lakes water. The answer welled up within me so fast that I impolitely didn't raise my hand to answer, as the moderator had instructed panel members to do.

"No one is trying to deny any citizens access to Great Lakes water," I said. "If they move here and live in the Great Lakes Basin they can have all the access to Great Lakes water they can possibly use."

At the end of the same discussion, a philosophy professor thoughtfully pointed out that water has a spiritual value and in many faiths the sharing of water is considered an act of humaneness. Although she was an opponent of exporting water from the Great Lakes, she wanted to know how those of us trying to protect the lakes from exportation could reconcile that with humanity's need for water for survival. Didn't we run the risk of appearing to hoard water that millions needed?

This time I did raise my hand and was acknowledged and permitted to answer. I first pointed to a clause of the proposed Great Lakes compact that exempted from its ban on exports any that are made "on a short-term basis for firefighting, humanitarian or emergency response purposes." In other words, to keep thirsty people from dying anywhere on earth, no one would oppose the short-term use of the Great Lakes.

Then I found other words—or they found me. I said that water has a spiritual value as part of a place, the place where it was put by the Creator. Great Lakes water is not water alone but the essential source of life for the humans who live here and a multitude of other living things that are part of a living system. Wasn't it risking arrogance to think we could simply take a large amount of it and put it elsewhere? How was that consistent with spirituality?

I convinced no one, but I was speaking with the force of all my heart.

CHAPTER 9

Water for Life, Not Profit

ARE THERE ANY circumstances under which the life-giving waters of the Great Lakes should be shared significantly with people outside the basin in which those waters are found? The answer, like most of adult life, is more complicated than it seems at first and more complicated than anyone wants it to be. But it can be reduced to this: for human survival, yes, but human survival does not include lawn and golf course watering in the desert, ornamental fountain filling at casinos, or the subsidization of homes and businesses where they have no reason to be located in an affluent society in which there is ample opportunity for human choice.

Too often in the last 25 years the rhetorical skirmishes over the future "sharing" of the Great Lakes have played out in public as Sunbelt greed versus Great Lakes hoarding. As a Michigan-born man I understand and share the visceral dislike of water exports from the Great Lakes to anywhere on earth and the resulting perception of outsiders that a colony of human water hogs inhabits the region. But no one has really asked the people of Michigan or any of their Great Lakes neighbors whether they are willing to relinquish some basin water to save human lives. If they were asked, I am confident a vast majority of them would say yes.

The closest we have come to this point is not very close. In 2005, when Hurricane Katrina walloped New Orleans and the adjoining Gulf shore, the Great Lakes water commercialization industry smelled an opportunity. The nation watched as helpless thousands lived in bestial conditions for days. In the late summer heat, elderly and vulnerable refugees slowly died awaiting medical attention, air-conditioning, food—and water.

On May 26, 2005, just over three months before, Michigan governor Jennifer M. Granholm had imposed (with boldness if questionable legal authority) a moratorium on new permits or approvals for bottled water processors "unless the applicant certifies that the delivery or sale of all bottled water production will be limited to the Great Lakes Basin. This temporary moratorium is intended to afford the Michigan legislature an opportunity to debate and enact a comprehensive water withdrawal law and legislation addressing the issue of what constitutes a diversion of Great Lakes water."[1]

Now thousands were in desperate need of potable water in New Orleans and nearby—water impossible for devastated municipal systems to supply. Would Michigan begrudge these people some Great Lakes Basin water?

Granholm moved with alacrity (and no public objections) to remove any appearance of a selfish water policy. On September 7, 2005, she issued a temporary suspension of the previous directive and ordered the Michigan Department of Environmental Quality "and other state departments and agencies . . . [to] take no action under Executive Directive 2005–5, Michigan law, or other regulations to inhibit or delay the provision of drinking water to assist in responding to the effects of Hurricane Katrina."[2] The new order made the problem clear: "within the area of the Gulf Coast region affected by Hurricane Katrina there is a critical need for drinkable water for both the victims of the storm and individuals engaged in relief efforts."

This was good symbolism, although it had no measurable effect on the provision of bottled water to New Orleans and its vicinity. The original May directive had also been symbolic, designed to put pressure on a balky legislature to pass some kind of water withdrawal legislation. No "permits or approvals" for bottled water processors were then pending, and none had entered the queue by September 2. But Michigan's chief executive removed any thought that the state was going to be inhumane about providing Great Lakes bottled water in an emergency.

Good thing, too; the industry had been quick to spot the opportunity inherent in the crisis. The International Bottled Water Association was able to reap rewards from its willingness to help.

The International Bottled Water Association (IBWA) has been honored by the American Society of Association Executives (ASAE) for three "Associations Advance America Awards" for 2006. . . . IBWA won the ASAE Award of Excellence for 2006 for its "Bottled Water Emergency Relief" program, which resulted in significant benefit to American society. IBWA provided information to ASAE about extraordinary IBWA member and staff efforts to provide bottled water relief supplies to survivors of Hurricane Katrina and other storms, as well as industry action in response to terrorist attacks of Sept. 11, 2001 and other drinking water emergency situations.[3]

The bottled water association itself boasted that it "was selected to receive the Award of Excellence out of nearly 100 entries for relief efforts after Hurricane Katrina. Rather than wait for the formal relief effort to become more organized, IBWA members and staff made direct contacts with officials and civic and municipal leagues in Katrina-affected towns and cities to provide bottled water to those in need."[4] While the quick action was surely helpful, it also had marketing benefits. And, at least for once, the environmental community and the bottled water industry agreed on something: if people were at risk of serious illness or death, no water basin boundary should stop the trucking or flight of bottles of water to aid them on an emergency basis.

As dramatic as the Katrina catastrophe and Granholm's directive was, it was also unique in the long-running fight over Great Lakes water exports. At no other time since the fight began had American citizens on such a mass scale been in need of emergency drinking water. One can only hope the disaster does not repeat itself in the future.

The unasked and unanswered question after Katrina was whether Michigan or any of the Great Lakes states would have been as quick to relax a Great Lakes export restriction for sufferers in South America, Africa, or Asia. And, barring further federal government incompetence on the scale seen after Hurricane Katrina, this is likely the next scenario in which Great Lakes water may become a humanitarian resource. For water scarcity abroad—threatening human survival—is likely to be a persistent theme of the twenty-first century. And such scarcity could last much longer than the post-Katrina weeks in which New Orleans residents languished.

In August 2006, the International Water Management Institute released its estimate that a full third of the world was facing water shortages. As one news agency described it, "Globally, water usage had increased by six times in the past 100 years and would double again by 2050, driven mainly by irrigation and demands by agriculture, said Frank Rijsberman, the institute's director-general. Billions of people in Asia and Africa already faced water shortages because of poor water management, he said."[5] Water scarcity in Australia and Asia was already affecting 1.5 billion people according to the institute.

The causes weren't as simple as a hotter, drier climate in most cases. The institute's employees, like other experts, pointed out that wasteful irrigation practices are tying up greater volumes of water. And in some areas of Africa, where water is in abundance, the wells, pumps and pipes needed to get it to people who need it are scarce or nonexistent.

Meanwhile, the affluent were using more than their "fair share." The World Wildlife Fund (WWF) reported in the same month that urban Australians were using an average of 300 liters of water daily and compared them to Europeans, who consumed about 200 liters, and people in sub-Saharan Africa, who existed on 10 to 20 liters a day.[6]

At home in the United States, the problem of waste is just as grave or worse. Burgeoning populations in the Southwest and either cyclical drought or climate change have tested the water supply of several states in the last decade. In April 2007, the *New York Times* noted that $2.5 billion in water projects were planned or under way in Nevada, California, Arizona, and New Mexico—a resurgence of expensive, managed water movement after decades of decline. One was a proposed 280-mile pipeline that would direct water to Las Vegas from northern Nevada.[7]

"The scramble for water," the *Times* reported, "is driven by the realities of population growth, political pressure and the hard truth that the Colorado River, a 1,400-mile-long silver thread of snowmelt and a lifeline for more than 20 million people in seven states, is providing much less water than it had." The paper added that some long-term projections based on climate change scenarios suggested that "mountain snows that feed the Colorado River will melt faster and evaporate in greater amounts with rising global temperatures, providing stress to the waterway even without drought."

There was a time not long ago when the economics of exporting Great

Lakes water to southwestern states seemed outlandish. Billions of dollars in engineering and construction costs—presumably borne by taxpayers—would be required, in part to pump water thousands of feet uphill. But that was before the commercial sale of water became a major industry. Suddenly the price of water by unit of volume—and the willingness of consumers to pay it voluntarily rather than being forced to shovel it out in taxes—took on a new dimension. As Jeffrey Potter of the Biodiversity Project wrote in September 2006:

> How would you feel if your water utility charged the same price as Coca-Cola, Pepsi, Nestlé and all the rest of the corporate water bottlers in the U.S.? I did a little math on this and here's what I found. The average cost of bottled water in the U.S. is about $1.27/gallon (this includes all bottled water products, large and small). Here in Madison, Wisconsin, the average person uses 75.3 US gallons of city water each day. If the city decided to charge the same price that commercial water bottlers charge, then a typical resident's water bill would jump from $0.10/day up to $95.63/day. In my house, that means my annual water bill from the city would jump from less than $300 to nearly $23,000.[8]

Clearly, such a price jump would spur a citizens' revolt in Madison or anywhere in the East. But, with a combination of subsidies and a greater willingness to pay, the price of exporting Great Lakes water might be closer to right. And under the looming Great Lakes interstate compact any amount of basin water could be shipped long distances by truck as long as it is packaged in individual containers with a volume of 5.7 gallons or less. And for what?

The answer has a lot to do with whether the definition of *humanitarian emergency* includes severe water shortages brought on by decades of human mucking around with hydrology in order to stimulate and then support unsustainable population growth in vast areas of the arid West. Anyone familiar with Marc Reisner's 1986 classic, *Cadillac Desert*, knows there is ample precedent for the movement of water vast distances with billions in federal subsidies. Reisner wrote, "Agricultural paradises were formed out of seas of sand and humps of rock. Sprawling cities sprouted out of nowhere. . . . The cost of all this, however, was a vandalization both of our natural heritage and our economic future, and the reckoning has not even begun." He asked who would pay the bill for dredging trillions of tons of silt out of faltering reservoirs or "to bring more water to whole regions, whole states, dependent on aquifers that have been recklessly mined?"[9]

Perhaps all of us who are U.S. taxpayers. The idea is not terribly far-fetched. Congress has a habit of dishing out billions of dollars in legal authorizations in its periodic updates of the Water Resources Development Act, the WRDA. Dubbed "a pork-barrel bill by design" by the National Wildlife Federation, the seven versions of WRDA enacted between 1986 and 2000 cost federal taxpayers an estimated $25.4 billion.[10] Only in recent times has WRDA made room for a few ecologically friendly investments such as a plan to restore the Florida Everglades included in the 2000 version.

In fact, supporters of the Great Lakes compact have called attention to another looming increase in congressional voting power for the Sunbelt states as a reason to rush ratification of the document by the eight states and Congress. Fearing that protection of the huge public investment in delivering water to Southwest cities and farms could result in further massive spending to export Great Lakes water, they point out that after the 2010 census, the eight states could hold only about 95 seats in the U.S. House, down from a high of 150 seats in 1930. Urging adoption of the compact by the Indiana legislature, the *South Bend Tribune* said the action should be prompt "and certainly before the 2010 census, when the Great Lakes basin could lose congressional representation because of a shift in the national population."[11]

True—but then there's that exemption from water in bottles and other small containers, the legal San Andreas fault that could drain the Great Lakes. Meanwhile, communities just outside the Great Lakes Basin but inside one of the Great Lakes states, continue to undermine the case for keeping Great Lakes water out of the hands of sprawl supporters. The most dramatic example continues to be Waukesha, Wisconsin, which has pleaded for the right to take millions of gallons of Lake Michigan water a day to keep its outside-the-basin luxury housing and commercial development going. As Emily Green of the Sierra Club said in 2005, "Yes, people need a place to live. . . . But do they need McMansions on five-acre lots?"[12]

What is clear today is that few in the Great Lakes region have begun to think in more than superficial terms about what will happen if there is an even more dramatic change in the climate of states that are home to millions of U.S. citizens. The bare words "humanitarian emergency" in the compact do not begin to address the issue. The politics could get interesting if some economist demonstrates that trucking Great Lakes water, or even building a pipeline, is more "cost effective" than a massive resettlement program of Sunbelters to the lush Great Lakes region.

Selling out conservation will not balance the budget or purge the legislature of special-interest/lobbyist-dictated corruption. That takes leadership and integrity that puts the public interest before the next election's Big Bucks donors. It takes being "owned" by what's good for the resource and people ahead of being "owned" by who will pump the most dollars into the campaign's coffers.

—Glen Sheppard, *North Woods Call,* July 2003

I don't know how long he intends to be the spokesman and advocate for the "real world" in the north woods: the spoiler of unrelenting development; the gentle critic of satisfied and self-important environmentalists; the defender of trout, trilliums, mayflies, and rivers; the nagging gadfly in Lansing's environmental politics; the joyful chronicler of dogs, grouse, and gameless hunts; the skillful teller of stories; the down-to-earth, gritty, let-it-all-hang-out reporter; and more. With all of the above, the "and more" is the most impressive . . .

So enjoy the curmudgeon of the drumlins while you can.

—Ed McGlinn, Anglers of the Au Sable, on Glen Sheppard

CHAPTER 10

Great Lakes Not for Sale

IN A CYNICAL AGE in which truth is less appealing than word choices that touch the chords of our hearts, while turning our attention from the lies these words conceal, how can those who love the Great Lakes fight to preserve them? How can we combat the spin that says we who oppose exporting these waters are being selfish, that we are being unreasonable, that we don't care about human survival? Should we come up with our own word choices? Or should we just follow our guts?

For the answer I turn not to the men and women who work in the political system (many of whom I respect deeply), and make a difference there, nor to professional communicators or public relations experts, who can also make a helpful difference. I turn instead to a bald guy with crazy eyes and a profane tongue who tutored me not long after I first got into conservation. His name is Glen Sheppard.

Months after I got the job as environmental policy adviser to the governor of Michigan in 1983, I knew I needed to pay homage to Shep, as he is known to all who love him even at his most maddening. As editor and publisher of the *North Woods Call*, a tabloid on Michigan outdoor issues read by often influential insiders—and a couple of thousand other laypersons who just love hunting and fishing—Shep was an institution by the early 1980s. He made no pretense of being an objective journalist. As a box on his editorial page says, the *Call* is dedicated to the proposition that there is only one side to any story involving the outdoors—nature's. He infuriated Lansing's natural resources bureaucrats not only by publishing things they didn't want to see in print but also by publishing things he supposed to be true that simply weren't. I could have disliked him, but I liked him instantly on meeting him.

I know he wasn't sure about me. He was skeptical of a conservation policy adviser to a governor who had never hunted or fished. The previous governor's adviser had been a vigorous sportsman.

He also knew that at the time I met him, and was advising the chief executive of the Michigan state government, I had less than one year of professional experience in conservation and only about three years total if you generously counted some volunteer work in the Sierra Club (of which he was no admirer).

We did have one thing in common that promoted bonding: we both liked whiskey. And, maybe more important, I liked listening to his tales of members of the World War II and Korean War generations who had come home from conflict; gotten training in what was then called fish, game, and forest management; and scattered into the fields and streams of Michigan to carry on a nascent conservation tradition. He was my teacher, and I was an eager student. At least I was wise enough to know how ignorant I was.

I stayed at the home he rented with his wife, Mary Lou, that weekend and two others in succeeding winters and springs. I'm not sure what we talked about on all the visits, but I know on the Saturday of my spring visit he packed me into his Suburban—a monstrous vehicle in which he carried his beloved hunting dogs and gear—and dropped me off on the Lake Michigan shore in a thick mist. He told me to walk south from the boundary of Fisherman's Island State Park and said that he would pick me up seven miles south. It was a test of sorts. I passed only in the sense that I am stubborn in a stupid sort of way, the course was not that tough, and only once did I hear voices that made me wonder if I was in the middle of the woods with some drug dealers. When Shep picked me up, in the classic tough guy mentor mode he neither complimented me nor commented on my seven-mile trek. The guy did not waste words—or emotions—except on his wife, his dogs, and the spectacular beauty of Michigan.

Over the years Shep and I drifted apart. As my governor continued to disappoint and then infuriate him with his conservation policies, Shep stopped talking to me and for a while I to him. Then a governor he disliked even more took office, throwing me into the private nonprofit sector, and we had common cause for dissatisfaction. But we didn't sip whisky together again.

What we did believe together—since he had passed it along to me from our first meeting—was that there are things in the natural world that are worth fighting for. And, just as important, Shep taught me, you cannot let yourself be cajoled, tricked, fooled, or reasoned out of that deep feeling in your belly that something more than your own interest or even that of your generation is at stake. In short, he taught me responsibility toward future generations.

Shep didn't introduce me to the natural world, although he fixed a few concepts in my consciousness. It's all about habitat, he'd say. If you don't conserve and protect habitat your work ain't worth a damn. Environmentalists and conservationists could look across their divide and occasionally see something familiar, and work together, he told me. And he also said, in words I would come to remember more clearly each year, a conservation commitment in a politician doesn't announce itself; it proves itself.

The guy could be prejudiced, mean-spirited and frequently ornery. And, interestingly, since he was my inspiration on the issue of commercializing the Great Lakes, he saw no big problem with water capture and sale per se. He thought it was silly, though; you should drink tap water, he editorialized. But environmentally, he said, the only problem with Nestlé's big dreams was their impact on the trout streams he loved.

But you know what? Shep could be wrong on an issue and still correct in his basic conservation instincts. Letting the Great Lakes go from a public trust resource to a commodity carved up by special interests is not something he would tolerate if he saw it the way it truly is. In that, Shep is like many other advocates I admire.

One of them, a man who participated in the 2006 Michigan legislative deal that declared water exported from the state in containers under 5.7 gallons in size is not a diversion, said it was too late to do anything about water commercialization. "Just go to any grocery store and look on the shelves—they've been selling bottled water for years."

But I know he missed the point.

This fight is not about bottled water.

This fight is not about economic protectionism.

This fight is not about hoarding or denying or even, in the end, keeping the Great Lakes as they are. Should some catastrophic need arise, few will stand in the way of an emergency transfusion of water to save lives far away. But under what terms, for whom, and for how long? The words "short-term humanitarian emergency" may be the most important yet least well-defined of the many in the Great Lakes compact. They deserve more consideration and thought. And the Great Lakes will definitely not stay the same: as they always have, they will continue to transform themselves.

The fight is about something much bigger than that. It is about democracy and the public interest. For *when* have the people, or their duly elected representatives at any level of government, after open debate in front of the citizenry and with full consciousness of their own actions, and with the assent of the same citizenry, authorized the taking of Great Lakes water for private profit by constitutional amendment, statute, or rule?

They have not as of this writing. And until they do the waters of the Great Lakes belong to all the people and are held in trust by the governments charged with protecting their interests.

In the last 25 years—approximately the amount of time that I have been either working inside or trying to influence various governments—the idea of "public trust" has been disparaged to the point of worthlessness. I have watched as ideologues of the Far Right have demonized the term *government*, equating it with *incompetence* and *arrogance*, first by smothering their opposition with these adjectives, then by demonstrating both incompetence and arrogance in their own management of government. It is a masterly dogma that proves itself through the duplicity and venality of its adherents.

In the case of the Great Lakes, and their governments, this degrading of government, public servants, and public trust has not quite yet cost us the lakes themselves. No amount of propaganda has yet overcome the visceral understanding of tens of millions of Americans and Canadians that, while private property is sacred, 18 percent of the world's available surface freshwater and the shores it laps are an even more solemn trust.

To date, no one has been able to cheapen the mystery and beauty of the Great Lakes through mere rhetoric. The steps that governments have taken toward relinquishing public control of the Great Lakes, in the sway of lobbyists, have occurred after dark, out of the public view. There has been no debate and no public decision anywhere that the Great Lakes can be commercialized—yet we are perilously close to that calamity. This is in part because the lobbyists and their sponsors have cloaked their rapacious dreams in words of reassurance and familiarity when a wrenching change of historic significance is imminent.

It is time for those who want to profit from the abundance of the Great Lakes to come out of hiding and put their proposition in front of the public in plain language. I do not believe they can win this debate, but let it occur. Let it be free, robust, direct yet respectful. Then let the public decide.

Let me make it clear again that this is not just a decision about bottled water. It is about whether the public will have a chance to decide whether the commercialization of its water is in the public interest. It is not too much to ask that the fate of a public trust be determined by the public that must decide how it wants to treat, and be remembered by, descendants for whom that trust is also held.

Great Lakes water is not to be used by the basin's inhabitants or defenders as a tool or a weapon. But neither is it booty or treasure in a conventional sense.

As the Lakes developed, their waters were considered (like many others) a common country because they enabled travel. The waters of the lakes and their tributaries were a major highway linking the Atlantic with the Northwest of both Canada and the United States. They were instrumental to the continent economically.

The right of free travel on those waters was sacred. But now we live in the twenty-first century. And needs have evolved. Some will say that means the lakes don't belong to all; they are up for grabs.

Others say this: the right of free travel on waters would have made no sense if the waters were drained away. In fact, the right would have been meaningless.

So even if you aren't swayed by the beauty of the lakes—think of the rights that reach back over 200 years.

And think of the public trust doctrine that reaches back to the Roman Empire.

There is wisdom behind these principles, and embedded in them, I believe, is also a powerful emotion.

These waters are not to be disturbed for anything but the most paramount human priorities. And the private profit of wealthy investors who have no personal stake in the lakes is not among those priorities.

Let it not be said that the people of the Great Lakes Basin gave away the lakes without a fight—or even a serious discussion.

Notes

PROLOGUE

1. This estimate is based on U.S. Census figures, which indicate a Great Lakes Basin population (in 2000–2001) of approximately 33 million and a global population (in early 2007) of 6.5 billion.

CHAPTER ONE

1. International Joint Commission, "Great Lakes Diversions and Consumptive Uses," January 1985, p. 82, http://www.ijc.org, accessed October 10, 2006.
2. Council of Great Lakes Governors, "Great Lakes Water Management Chronology Key Events," http://www.cglg.org, accessed October 11, 2006.

CHAPTER TWO

1. Tom Hundley, "Mississippi Boat Traffic Shut Down," *Chicago Tribune*, June 23, 1988.
2. Barbara Stanton, "Great Lakes States Split about Water," *Detroit Free Press*, June 29, 1988.
3. Robert Irion, "Four Governors Oppose Thompson Water Plan," *Chicago Tribune*, June 24, 1988.
4. "Great Lakes: Draining off Would Set a Troubling Precedent," *Detroit Free Press*, June 30, 1988.
5. Another section of the law contained a clause that exempted "any diversion of water from any of the Great Lakes which is authorized on the date of the enactment of this Act," which was November 17, 1986.
In September 2000, Congress amended WRDA to ban water *exports* also unless consented to by all eight governors (42 USC 1962d-20(d)). The word *bulk* as a lim-

itation on "export" was rejected (James M. Olson, *Navigating the Great Lakes Compact: Water, Public Trust, and International Trade Agreements*, 2006 Michigan State Law Review 1103, 1122 [2006]).

6. As of 2007, Pleasant Prairie had not announced any plan to end its "temporary" diversion.

7. Brendan O'Shaugnessey, "Indiana Towns Shut Out While Chicago Suburbs Flourish," *Northwest Indiana Times*, December 13, 2004.

8. Although Engler won in a landslide that November, his Democratic opponent, Geoffrey Fieger, accused Engler of being "the first Michigan governor to agree to the diversion of water out of the Great Lakes." John Flesher, "Fieger Blasts Engler on Swing through the North," *Traverse City Record-Eagle*, October 9, 1998.

9. Peter Annin, *The Great Lakes Water Wars* (Washington, D.C.: Island Press, 2006), 198.

10. James S. Lochhead, Chad G. Asarch, Milos Birutciski, Patrick J. Monahan, Gray E. Taylor, Pieter M. Schenkkan, "Report to the Council of Great Lakes Governors: Governing the Withdrawal of Water from the Great Lakes," May 18, 1999, 4.

11. Chris A. Shafer to G. Tracy Mehan III, Director, Office of the Great Lakes, Michigan Department of Environmental Quality, July 7, 1999.

12. Chris A. Shafer, *Great Lakes Diversions Revisited: Legal Constraints and Opportunities for State Regulation*, 17 Thomas M. Cooley Law Review 461 (2000).

13. "Report to the Council of Great Lakes Governors," 17.

14. U.S. Army Engineer Research and Development Center, Waterways Experiment Station, Environmental Laboratory, Vicksburg, "Ecological Effects of Water Level Reductions in the Great Lakes Basin: Report on a Technical Workshop, December 16–17, 1999."

15. James M. Olson, *The Public Trust Doctrine: Procedural and Substantive Limitations on the Governmental Reallocation of Natural Resources in Michigan*, 1975 Detroit College of Law Review 163 (1975).

16. James T. Paul, "The Public Trust Doctrine: Who Has the Burden of Proof?" paper presented at the meeting of the Western Association of Wildlife and Fisheries Administrators, July 1996.

17. Alison Rieser, *Ecological Preservation as a Public Property Right: An Emerging Doctrine in Search of a Theory*, 15 Harvard Environmental Law Review 393 (1991).

18. Chris L. Shafer, "Great Lakes Diversions Revisited: Legal Constraints and Opportunities for State Regulation," report prepared for the National Wildlife Federation, 43–44 (2000).

19. 211 N.W. 115, 118 (Mich. 1926).

20. Olson, *Navigating the Great Lakes Compact*, 1130.

CHAPTER THREE

1. Felicia Thomas-Lynn, "Perrier Shelves Its Plan for State: Company Shifts to Michigan for Water Bottling Plant," *Milwaukee Journal Sentinel*, May 10, 2001.

2. Michigan Land Use Institute, "Michigan's Attorney General Weighs In: Perrier Project Is a Great Lakes Diversion," https://www.mlui.org, accessed November 27, 2007.

3. Jennifer M. Granholm, "Attorney General's Opinion on Perrier and Water Diversion," Michigan Land Use Institute, https://www.mlui.org, accessed November 27, 2007.

4. Terry Swier, "A David and Goliath Battle for Water Protection," *Great Lakes Aquatic Habitat News* 9, no. 6, (November–December 2001).

5. Opinion, State of Michigan, 49th Judicial Circuit, Mecosta County Circuit Court, *Michigan Citizens for Water Conservation et al. v. Nestlé Waters North America Inc.*, Case no. 01–14563–CE, Hon. Lawrence C. Root, Presiding, http://www.en vlaw.com, accessed November 27, 2007.

6. "Judge Rules Again in Favor of Michigan Citizens for Water Conservation," news release, Michigan Citizens for Water Conservation, December 9, 2003, http://www.savemiwater.org, accessed November 27, 2007.

7. "Granholm Calls for Comprehensive Water Use Statute: DEQ, DLEG Directors File Amicus Brief on Behalf of Mecosta County Workers," news release, Michigan Department of Environmental Quality, December 16, 2003, http://www.michigan.gov, accessed February 23, 2007.

8. "Griffin Forum Highlights Concerns about Survival of the Great Lakes," *Central Michigan Life*, April 20, 2005.

CHAPTER FOUR

1. Jeff Alexander, "Nestlé's Raises Stakes in Bottled Water Battle," *Muskegon Chronicle*, January 7, 2007.

2. Charles Ferguson Barker, *The Day the Great Lakes Drained Away* (Traverse City, Mich.: Mackinac Island Press, 2005).

3. Mackinac Island Press Web site, http://www.mackinacislandpress.com.

4. "Great Lakes Basin Water Resources Compact," draft, May 20, 2005, copy in author's possession.

5. "Great Lakes Basin Water Resources Compact," draft, October 9, 2005, copy in author's possession.

6. National Wildlife Federation, "Memorandum to Great Lakes Environmental and Conservation Organizations," October 10, 2005, copy in author's possession.

7. "Great Lakes–St. Lawrence River Basin Water Resources Compact," December 13, 2005, copy in author's possession.

8. Ibid.

9. Canadian Legal Information Institute, International Boundary Waters Treaty Act and associated regulations, http://www.canlii.org, accessed October 30, 2006.

10. Michigan Citizens for Water Conservation, "Proposed Great Lakes Plan Would Convert Water into Product for Export," news release, November 22, 2005, copy in author's possession.

11. Hiroshi and Arlene Kanno to Governor James Doyle, November 18, 2005, copy in author's possession.

12. Deb Price, "Thirsty States May Covet Lakes' Water," *Detroit News*, August 14, 2005.

13. John Flesher, "Bottled Water Exports OK under Proposed Compromise," Associated Press, October 12, 2005.

14. Great Lakes United, press release, December 12, 2005, copy in author's possession.

15. Council of Canadians, media release, December 13, 2005, copy in author's possession.

16. "Great Lakes, Great Michigan: Stop the No Rules Water Grab," undated fact sheet, copy in author's possession.

17. E-mail message from Clean Water Action to members of the Great Lakes, Great Michigan coalition, February 8, 2006, copy in author's possession.

18. Personal communication from Jim Olson, February 10, 2006.

19. "State Right to Regulate Water Withdrawals," *Battle Creek Enquirer*, editorial, February 14, 2005.

CHAPTER FIVE

1. Angela Goebel Bain, Lynne Manring, and Barbara Mathews, Memorial Hall Museum Online, American Centuries . . . View from New England, "Native Peoples in New England," http://www.memorialhall.mass.edu, accessed October 24, 2006.

2. Big Ox, "The Power of Oxygen," http://www.thebigox.com, accessed October 24, 2006.

3. Mike Murphy, "Water Authority Wants Privately Owned Well: Townships Say Aquifer Satisfies Regional Needs," *Detroit News*, February 21, 2002.

4. Saul Landau, "The Privatization of Everything: Reagan and Bottled Water," Counterpunch, August 27–28, 2005, http://www.counterpunch.org, accessed October 24, 2006.

5. Stephen Hesse, "A Craze from Marketing Heaven: Bottled Water and Problems That Flow," *Japan Times*, August 23, 2006.

6. John Myers, "A Group Urges Northlanders to Stop Drinking Bottled Water, Saying It Leads to Pollution and Wastes Energy," *Duluth News Tribune*, April 12, 2006.

7. A commercial water filter manufacturer, Aquasana, featured these quotes on its Web site, http://www.aquasanastore.com, accessed November 27, 2007.

8. Environmental Working Group, "More Than 140 Contaminants with No Enforceable Safety Limits Found in Nation's Drinking Water," news release, December 20, 2005, http://www.ewg.org, accessed March 23, 2007.

9. Natural Resources Defense Council, "Bottled Water: Pure Drink or Pure Hype?" http://www.nrdc.org, accessed March 22, 2007.

10. International Bottled Water Association, "Bottled Water Regulations: Questions and Answers," http://www.bottledwater.org, accessed March 22, 2007.

11. CBC News, "Buying Bottled Water Is Wrong, Suzuki Says: Environmentalist Launches National Tour on Green Issues," February 1, 2007, http://www.cbc.ca, accessed March 23, 2007.

12. Donald Roy, personal communication, October 10, 2006.

13. Beverage Marketing Corporation, "Bottled Water Continues Tradition of

Strong Growth in 2005, Beverage Marketing Corporation Reports: Second Largest Category Leads Beverage Categories in Volume Growth," news release, April 2006, copy in author's possession.

14. Myra P. Saefong, "Water's a Precious Commodity, So Why Isn't It Traded on an Exchange like Oil?" Dow Jones Marketwatch, June 30, 2006, http://www.marketwatch.com, accessed November 27, 2007.

CHAPTER SIX

1. A testimonial to Marion's work to end war and information about an endowed fund for peace activists established in her name by her family at Oberlin College can be found on the Oberlin Web site, http://www.oberlin.edu, accessed November 27, 2007.

2. See, for example, Environmental Health Coalition, Border Environmental Justice Campaign, http://www.environmentalhealth.org/maquiladoras, accessed April 6, 2007. The statement reads, "The maquiladora program was designed to bring jobs and prosperity to northern cities, while at the same time providing cheap labor for foreign owned manufacturers. Although the program has produced jobs, the work typically involves low wages (the average worker earns about $4.80 a day), few benefits, little job security, and high exposure to toxics. In 1997 the maquiladoras employed more than 900,000 people working at more than 3,000 plants, mainly along the border."

3. World Trade Organization, "Trade Resources: History," http://www.wto.org, accessed April 11, 2007.

4. World Trade Organization, "Trade Resources: History: GATT," http://www.wto.org, accessed April 11, 2007.

5. See http://www.eco-pros.com, accessed April 10, 2007.

6. Forum on Democracy and Trade, http://www.forumdemocracy.net, accessed April 10, 2007.

7. Claudia H. Deutsch, "There's Money in Thirst," *New York Times*, August 10, 2006.

8. Council of Canadians, "Bush Announcement Ends Myth That Canada's Water Is Safe from Bulk Export," news release, July 18, 2001, http://www.canadians.org, accessed March 29, 2006. See also Tom Henry, "Canada Vehemently Rejects Idea of Water Exports: Casual Remark by President Bush Sparks Flurry of Editorial Comment across Country," *Pittsburgh Post-Gazette*, July 21, 2001.

9. Paul Muldoon, Executive Director, Canadian Environmental Law Association, "The Case against Water Exports," March 2000, http://www.elements.nb.ca, accessed November 27, 2007.

10. Jeff Fleischer, "Blue Gold: An Interview with Maude Barlow," *Mother Jones*, January 14, 2005.

11. Diane Francis, "Time to Tap Canada's Water Riches: We Should Ignore Left-Wing Bleating and Exploit This Renewable Resource," *Financial Post*, September 27, 2006.

12. Maude Barlow and Tony Clarke, "The Battle for Water," AlterNet, December 9, 2003, http://www.alternet.org, accessed November 27, 2007.

13. International Joint Commission, "Protection of the Waters of the Great Lakes: Interim Report to the Governments of the United States and Canada," sec. 1: "Introduction," http://www.ijc.org, accessed April 6, 2007.

14. International Joint Commission, "Protection of the Waters of the Great Lakes: Final Report to the Governments of the United States and Canada," http://www.ijc.org, accessed April 7, 2007.

15. Remarks by Frank Ettawageshik, Chair, Little Traverse Bay Band, Odawa Indians, December 4, 2004, at a ceremony hosted by the Environmental Protection Agency to kick off a collaborative initiative to devise a plan to restore the Great Lakes.

16. Craig Bowron, "More Powerful Than We Imagine," *Minneapolis Star Tribune*, April 6, 2007.

17. Brian McKenna, "Great Lakes for Sale! Michigan's Odawa Indians Lead Anti-Nestlé Fight," *The Free Press*, April 22, 2006, http://freepress.org, accessed November 11, 2007.

CHAPTER SEVEN

1. Also known as "The Great Lakes Charter Annex: A Supplementary Agreement to the Great Lakes Charter," the document is available online at http://cglg.org, accessed April 17, 2007.

2. Section 4.13 also identifies two exemptions from the no-diversion language: "To supply vehicles, including vessels and aircraft, whether for the needs of the persons or animals being transported or for ballast or other needs related to the operation of the vehicles"; and "To use in a non-commercial project on a short-term basis for firefighting, humanitarian, or emergency response purposes."

3. Bob Kelleher, "Minnesota Considers Plan to Keep Great Lakes Water in the Great Lakes," Minnesota Public Radio, February 11, 2007, http://minnesota .publicradio.org, accessed April 30, 2007.

4. "Ohio Lawmakers' Hypotheticals Stall Effort to Protect Great Lakes," U.S. Water News Online, http://www.uswaternews.com, accessed April 30, 2007.

5. Aaron Marshall, "Legislator Holding Up Great Lakes Water Pact," *Cleveland Plain Dealer*, December 11, 2006.

6. Sam Speck, memorandum to Ohio senators, "RE: Great Lakes Compact Legislation–HB 574," December 11, 2006, copy in author's possession.

CHAPTER EIGHT

1. Ed White, "Engler Aide Warned Perrier Could Undermine Effort to Save Water," *Grand Rapids Press*, May 15, 2001.

2. Brad Heath, "Bottled-Water Dispute Could Weaken Control of Lakes," *Detroit News*, August 14, 2005.

3. "Nestlé Looks to Evart for More Water Wells," *Mt. Pleasant Morning Sun*, March 8, 2005.

4. Edward Hoogterp, *"Tapped In: Evart Sits on Precious Commodity,"* *Grand Rapids Press*, November 4, 2007.

5. Jeff Alexander, "River Lovers Take a Stand against Bottler," *Muskegon Chronicle*, March 30, 2007.

CHAPTER NINE

1. Governor Jennifer M. Granholm, State of Michigan Executive Directive 2005–5, "Temporary Moratorium on Bottled Water Permits and Approvals," May 26, 2005, http://michigan.gov, accessed June 22, 2007.

2. Governor Jennifer M. Granholm, State of Michigan Executive Directive 2005–8, "Temporary Suspension of Executive Directive 2005–5 for Provision of Bottled Water to Assist in Hurricane Katrina Relief Efforts," September 7, 2005, http://michigan.gov, accessed June 22, 2007.

3. The Water Connoisseur, "International Bottled Water Association Honored for Hurricane Relief," January 2006, http://www.finewaters.com, accessed June 22, 2007.

4. International Bottled Water Association, "IBWA Honored by American Society of Association Executives," news release, http://www.waterwebster.com, accessed June 22, 2007.

5. James Grubel, "Billions Face Water Shortages, Crisis Looms: Agency," Reuters, August 16, 2006, http://www.commondreams.org, accessed June 22, 2007.

6. ABC News On Line, "Wealth No Barrier to Water Crisis: WWF," August 16, 2007, http://www.abc.net, accessed June 22, 2007.

7. Randal C. Archibold and Kirk Johnson, "No Longer Waiting for Rain, an Arid West Takes Action," *New York Times*, April 4, 2007.

8. Jeffrey Potter, "Addicted to Water?" September 11, 2006, Great Lakes Town Hall, http://greatlakestownhall.org, accessed June 23, 2007.

9. Marc Reisner, *Cadillac Desert: The American West and Its Disappearing Water* (New York: Penguin, 1986), 484.

10. National Wildlife Federation, "What Is WRDA?" http://www.nwf.org, accessed June 23, 2007.

11. "Let's Approve Great Lakes Compact," *South Bend Tribune*, editorial, February 4, 2007.

12. Felicity Barringer, "If Waukesha Gets Water, Will Las Vegas Be Next?" *New York Times*, reprinted in *Duluth News Tribune*, August 15, 2005.

Index

About the Author

DAVE DEMPSEY is an environmental policy consultant and writer active in conservation for more than 25 years. He currently serves as Communications Director for Conservation Minnesota, a nonprofit organization in Minneapolis, and as an environmental policy and communications consultant for other organizations in Michigan and Minnesota.

Dave has been active in environmental matters since 1982. He served as Environmental Adviser to Michigan Governor James J. Blanchard from 1983 to 1989. From 1991 to 1994, Dave was Program Director at Clean Water Action. He served as Policy Director of the Michigan Environmental Council from 1994 to 1999. President Clinton appointed him to the Great Lakes Fishery Commission in 1994, where he served until 2001.

Dave is the author of *Ruin and Recovery: Michigan's Rise as a Conservation Leader* (2001), an environmental history of Michigan since its statehood in 1837, described by George Weeks of the *Detroit News* as "a remarkable book." He also wrote *On the Brink: The Great Lakes in the 21st Century*, a history of and commentary on the state of the world's largest freshwater ecosystem (2004), and a biography of Michigan's longest-serving governor,

William G. Milliken: Michigan's Passionate Moderate (2006). The *Grand Rapids Press* said this "excellent biography . . . reminds us that the original purpose of politics was to serve the people—not the candidates, not the pollsters, not the political consultants and backroom ideologues, and certainly not the political parties themselves."

Dave has a bachelor of arts degree from Western Michigan University and a master's degree in resource development from Michigan State University and served from 1999 to 2004 as an adjunct instructor at MSU in environmental policy through the Department of Resource Development (now Community, Agriculture, Recreation and Resource Studies). He serves on the board of directors of the nonprofit Alliance for the Great Lakes, which is based in Chicago.

Dave resides with his wife, Jennifer, in the Twin Cities metropolitan area of Minnesota.

Text design by Jillian Downey
Typesetting by Delmastype, Ann Arbor, Michigan
Text font: Janson
Display font: Trade Gothic Condensed No. 18

Although designed by the Hungarian Nicholas Kis in about 1690, the model for Janson Text was mistakenly attributed to the Dutch printer Anton Janson. Kis' original matrices were found in Germany and acquired by the Stempel foundry in 1919. This version of Janson comes from the Stempel foundry and was designed from the original type; it was issued by Linotype in digital form in 1985.

—courtesy www.adobe.com

The first cuts of Trade Gothic were designed by Jackson Burke in 1948, and he continued to work on further weights and styles until 1960.

—courtesy www.myfonts.com